THE JOURNEY TOWARDS RELEVANCE

—Simple Steps For Transforming Your World—

THE
JOURNEY TOWARDS
RELEVANCE

— Simple Steps For Transforming Your World —

Kary Oberbrunner

Published by Relevant Books
A division of Relevant Media Group, Inc.

www.relevant-books.com
www.relevantmediagroup.com

Design by Relevant Solutions
Cover and Interior Design by Mark Arnold

Library of Congress Control Number: 2003116893
International Standard Book Number: 0-9729276-8-9

For information or bulk orders:
RELEVANT MEDIA GROUP, INC.
POST OFFICE BOX 951127
LAKE MARY, FL 32795
407-333-7152

04 05 06 07 9 8 7 6 5 4 3 2 1

Printed in the United States of America

FOR KELLY

my friend, my soul mate, my lover
you are a true transformist

ACKNOWLEDGMENTS

"IF I HAVE SEEN FURTHER, IT IS BECAUSE I HAVE STOOD ON THE SHOULDERS OF GIANTS."

—Sir Isaac Newton

MY SOUL mate Kelly. You taught me how to fly and continue to help me steer. I thank God for the balance you bring. My family, the Oberbrunners, who corporately modeled how to see with eyes of faith (Mike, Linda, Kim, Sarah, and Jeremy). My other family, the Hoppes, who warmly invited and accepted me in spite of all my quirks (Mike, June, Michele, and Emily).

Carl Muenzmaier. You believed in me during some of my darkest hours. Jo Anne Muenzmaier. You believed in Carl during his. Brian Rants. We had to walk through the gray together. It was worth it. We've reached some pretty deep levels together. Johnny Schatzman. One of the first transformists I ever met. Nate Siebert, Kevin Buettner, and Chad Nelson. Shall I begin with our tales of tyranny? My grandparents still with me, Don and Millie Oberbrunner, and those who have gone before, Dan and Ginny Schatzman.

My coach Chet Scott, a punk in his own right, one who definitely keeps me laughing and learning. Gary Underwood. Football, lime chips, Tekken, our bond is much stronger than miles. Some of my mentors I met along the journey: Dr. Dave Plaster, Dr. Ron Manahan, Dr. Tom Edgington, Roger Peugh, Dr. Mark Soto, Dr. Ken Bickel, Jack Rants, Ernie Richards, and Larry Chamberlain.

Those who taught me to think so much it actually hurt: Dr. Skip Forbes, Dr. Herb Bateman, and Tim Moore. Those women who nurtured my spirit: Jill Uceny, and Dr. Tammy Schultz. And those who nurtured my hunger to write: Miss Bristol and Dr. Paulette Sauders.

The Schatzmans, my other family growing up. John, Nancy, John and Carrie, Jason, Chris and Marnia, and Andrea, I will always remember Brookfield, July 5th, and the day we sold used fireworks.

The buddies who tremendously impacted my life simply by being themselves: Matt Groen, Tim Wright, Scott Feather, Jason Knapp, Chris Darland, Wade Sutton, Aaron Luse, Andy Royer, Joel Walker, and Mike Myers. The notorious freshman floor ... beta 1st north (P1 N) and some of its residents (a few of whom were already mentioned): Andy Saunders, Dean Avey, Luke Fields, Josh Sprague, Andy Brightbill, Matt Vosberg, Josh Holt, Josh Walden, Tom Johns, Dan Tupps, Jeff Wike, and Ben Shoup.

The best pastoral team in the country: Rick Nuzum, Ed Jackson, Jeff Martin, Sean Spoelstra, and Phil Stoll. Marc Gegner, my friend and weekly warrior who asks me the tough questions. Dustin Godshall, for gifting me some of the air to breathe in order to write.

Several pastors who have modeled a balanced path for me: Dr. Bill Rudd, Mark Palmer, Mike Jentes, and Gary Richard.

The two beloved church bodies that took a chance on me: Tiosa Brethren Church and Powell Grace Brethren Church. The Fellowship of Grace Brethren Churches (FGBC), may you continue to seek a balanced view of culture and your role in it. The adult volunteers, student leaders, and teens in the Student Ministries program at Powell. You are a major inspiration to me.

To Misti May and Catherine Franco (and those previously mentioned) who were part of the test audience for this book. A special thanks to Chad Dutka for his friendship and consultation through some tough times in this process. Cara Davis for her time and vision invested in the mission of this book. To Cameron Strang and the team at RELEVANT. Our paths were meant to cross. Because ... our generation was meant for this message just as much as this message was meant for our generation.

The One who is the source of all original thought. You are the Only Way, the Infinite Truth, and the Abundant Life. A big HOORAY for the Trinity.

CONTENTS

PREFACE

WE'VE KILLED our most strategic evangelistic tool. Not only is it the most strategic, but it's fully endorsed and commanded by our Savior and Lord Jesus Christ. We spend millions of hours and dollars dreaming up other innovative ways on how to competently share our faith. We applaud our laborious efforts while we overlook employing the one proven method. We, the Universal Church of Christ, have failed to love one another.

> By this all men will know that you are My disciples,
> if you have love for one another.
> —*John 13:35*

The Church has been ripped apart and reassembled into two main camps that at best casually tolerate each other. If we are honest, these two groups are far from loving one another. In fact, more accurately, many individuals within these camps violently hate each other. Oh, they might not admit it, but it often comes out in off-handed comments, many times mentioned in gossip groups.

What are these camps? What types of people make up these groups? The first camp separates itself from people, society, and culture for the main purpose of remaining unstained by the world. This group takes the commands of God, which are not burdensome, and makes hundreds of other rules and laws in order to maintain personal holiness.[1] This camp judges all others by the man-made religion they have created. This camp is laced with fear: fear of sinning, fear of compromising, fear of enjoying anything in the world. These people are the separatists.

The second camp conforms itself to the ideals, philosophies, and goals of the world. They value what it values. They model what it models. They worship what it worships. They are a cookie cutter image of pop culture. In an attempt to be all things to all people and enjoy what God has created, they become enslaved to the created and an offense to fellow believers. They label others less liberated as backward and legalistic. They flaunt their freedom and condemn others for their disciplined lifestyle. These people are the conformists.

Each camp and every individual within these two camps has wounded others. Likewise, they've been wounded themselves. Both camps, because of their behavior, have become completely irrelevant. The self-deceived separatist camp justifies its behavior because of its love for God. The self-deceived conformist camp justifies its behavior because of its love for people. Imbalance, not love, characterizes both camps.

As a result, the Bride of Christ, the Church, lies wounded in the gutter of irrelevance.[2] The watching world that is supposed to see our love for each other only sees wounds and irrelevance. Instead of fulfilling our task of being salt and light, we appear dim and tasteless.[3]

There is a paradigm shift arising. There is an alternative beginning to be born. The remnant is assembling. These relevant individuals, who we'll call transformists—the ones who balance faith and culture with loving God and loving people—are emerging with steady force.

If the Church ever hopes to wake from its slumber of irrelevance, if it longs to turn its focus outward, away from the internal civil war brought on by separatists and conformists, then three things must happen.

The first thing that must take place is a crystal clear conversation that accurately and biblically defines relevance. Fuzzy thinking, perpetuated by separatists and conformists, has thus far dominated this argument. Believers are not sure what being relevant is or if they want to be defined by it, since no one truly understands its meaning. This fog of tension needs to be traveled through. We need to define and move through the gray if we ever hope to come to a place where we integrate our faith with our culture.

The second thing that must take place is healing. I'm not talking about surface healing. I'm referring to raw, no holds barred, authentic recovery—the type of healing that follows a pattern of defining the wound, approaching the pain, validating the offense, and then, and only then, healing the wound.

The wounds inflicted by separatists and conformists go deep. Some have resulted from years of legalism reinforced by shame and performance. Other wounds have been caused by raw addictions that have produced seasons of powerless spirituality. In any case, the Church can't move forward into displaying authentic love in its current state of fragmentation and wounded existence.

Third, we must examine the factors that contribute to the worldview of the transformist. We must explore and unwrap the defining characteristics, habits, and disciplines that embody the person who lives on the fine line of being in the world but not of it. This final component of the journey explicitly guides the reader through an intentional analysis of how to consume and discern media in a relevant yet biblical fashion. It moves through the fog and offers a road map toward maintaining a transformed mind.

The world needs a plethora of transformists. It needs a gathering of committed believers who thoughtfully balance faith and culture. What is your part? The choice is up to you. Are you willing to take the first step in the long journey?

CHAPTER 1 =

EDEN AGAIN

"THE ONLY THING NECESSARY FOR THE TRIUMPH OF EVIL IS FOR GOOD MEN TO DO NOTHING."

—*Edmund Burke*

ONE ORDINARY Thursday afternoon, a little over two years ago, my wife kidnapped me from work for my twenty-fifth birthday surprise. She just stopped by and told me at (toy) gunpoint to get into the car. Then, for the next hour and a half, she drove us on random roads somewhere in the middle of Ohio. We passed through the city, the country, and then through the middle of nowhere. We stopped on our way to visit some state parks that had some breathtaking natural rock formations.

You should've heard me. Every five minutes I asked, "Where are we going?" In fact, it annoys me now just thinking about how many times I uttered that question. Before you diagnose me as a control freak, you have to understand that I just like to know where I'm going. Surprises are great, but I prefer to have a general perception of where I am headed.

That Thursday evening, we arrived at a bed and breakfast castle. After a long winding road, we parked the car and walked past a collection of tiny cottages on our way to the castle. We gave the knight in shinning armor our hellos and checked into our room. We enjoyed a winter weekend of meals in the Grand Hall and cozy chats next to the fireplace. It was a journey worth remembering.

I suppose, as a reader, I have the same preference of wanting to know where I'm headed. I avoid an author who throws me in the car and takes me for a wild ride. I love an adventure, but you better tell me our proposed destination. I know and expect there to be curves in the road, detours in the journey, and surprises along the way, but I just want to understand the general direction I'm headed.

As your author, I want to tell you exactly where we're headed. God has many surprises for you along the way, I'm sure of that. There will be detours, curves, and maybe even a roadblock or two you will have to cross if you have the courage to do so. However, our ultimate destination is a transformed mind.

> *And do not be conformed to this world,*
> *but be transformed by the renewing of your mind.*
> *—Romans 12:2*

The irony of this verse is that although we're obviously expected to live within the world, we're told not to conform to the world. At first glance, I see this as God setting us up to fail. It smells a lot like the Garden of Eden.[1]

And the LORD God commanded the man, saying,
"From any tree of the garden you may eat freely; but from the tree of
the knowledge of good and evil you shall not eat, for in the day
that you eat from it you shall surely die."
—*Genesis 2:16-17*

In other words, go ahead Adam, skip around the nice garden. Have fun. Enjoy yourself. Even though I've created you immortal, I expect that for all eternity, you will not eat of the forbidden tree. That's all I ask. Can you do it?

I don't know about you, but I'm bound to do one of two things. The first thing I might do is head straight for the tree. Well, maybe I'd wait around for a few hundred years and then eat of the tree, but I would still eat of the tree.

Why? I'm not sure. I guess it's just in us all to take the easy way out. Why spend time resisting? Why expend the mental and emotional energy to fight the battle? It's a lot easier to conform to temptation. This first response characterizes the behavior of a conformist.

The other thing I might do is model the behavior of a separatist. If I acted like a separatist, I'd add to God's command. All God asked Adam was to not eat of the tree. If I'm thinking like a separatist, I'd add that I couldn't touch the fruit. I'd then build a fence around that particular tree. Next, I would refrain from eating any fruit from any tree because it would remind me of the forbidden fruit. If I still lusted after it, I'd make a rule that I can't talk or be near to my wife because she may bring up the forbidden tree in our conversation. Eventually, I'd realize it's just easier not to struggle, so I wouldn't allow myself to set foot in the garden at all.

These great man-made rules I'd create would be so brilliant that I'd hold my wife, or anyone else, to a standard of observing my personal rules. If they would refrain from obeying my personal rules, touching the fruit, speaking about the forbidden fruit, or failing to build a fence, then I'd condemn and judge them to be less spiritual than I am. I'd elevate my own rules as a type of judge and jury whereby I'd sentence all others to a crime of worldliness.

Through my attempts to not eat the fruit, I would have broken several of God's other POSITIVE commands that He gave to me, such as: be fruitful, multiply, fill the earth, and eat freely from any other tree![2]

Evidently, Eve struggled with this as well. She was on the fast track to imitating my grandiose plan of avoiding the forbidden tree. Notice Eve's response to the serpent. Remember that God commanded Adam not to eat from the tree of the knowledge of good and evil.[3] Because Scripture does not say that bad communication (Adam transferring God's command to Eve) was the first sin, I'm assuming Eve accurately heard Adam's restatement of God's command.[4] Therefore, based on her reply to the serpent, it's obvious Eve added to God's command:

> *And the woman said to the serpent,*
> *"From the fruit of the trees of the garden we may eat;*
> *but from the fruit of the tree which is in the middle of the garden,*
> *God has said, 'You shall not eat from it or touch it, lest you die.'"*[5]
> —*Genesis 3:2-3*

Did you catch it? Eve added to God's command by relaying to the serpent that she and Adam could not touch the fruit either. Eve, in my opinion a separatist, exhibited one of the two irrelevant extremes with which every living person constantly struggles. Although she eventually sinned, which all separatists do, she initially responded to the temptation, seen in her reply to the serpent, by adding to God's command.

Whereas Eve exhibited the tendencies of a separatist, Adam exhibited those of a conformist. He consciously conformed to temptation and to Eve's example. For a brief moment in time, Eve, the only other human alive, had eaten the fruit. Adam, although we are not told for how long, was in a position of resisting temptation. Everyone else in the world gave in, and he had the choice to not conform. You know the story. He conformed.

In today's world, as in throughout all history, a separatist is one who, because he is motivated by fear, does three things. First, he withdraws from the world. Second, he adds to God's commands. Third, he categorizes all activities as spiritual or secular. This behavior is a personal attempt, in one's own fleshly strength, to control temptation, sin, and holiness. In his attempt for personal holiness through his own strength, he just suppresses his sinfulness and breaks God's commands in other areas.

On the other hand, the conformist counts his losses and enjoys the pleasures of sin. He knows he is beat, so he doesn't waste any time. No need to show restraint, he might as well eat, drink, and be merry, for tomorrow he might die. Besides, to critically think through how to biblically discern culture takes way too much time and effort. Thus, the conformist does what he does best. He conforms.

> **BOTH THE SEPARATIST AND THE CONFORMIST ARE IMMERSED IN SIN. IS IT ANY DIFFERENT IN OUR DAY AND AGE?**

Choose your flavor; both the separatist and the conformist are immersed in sin. Is it any different in our day and age? Are separatists and conformists a thing of the past? Have we evolved so much in our spirituality that we no longer inherently struggle with the tendency to gravitate toward one of these two irrelevant extremes?

Have we deviated from the Eden scenario? After all, are we not commanded, in the high priestly prayer of our Lord and Savior Jesus, to be in the world and not of it?[6] It's as if God has said to us, "Go. Enjoy yourselves. Feel free to eat of culture. Partake in the fruit the world offers. Only do not eat of the forbidden fruit. For in that day you will die."

At least Adam and Eve knew what tree not to eat from. In our situation, most of us are clueless as to what tree kills.[7] This only complicates our dilemma. We're expected to enjoy the world God created, yet most of us live life without specifically knowing which trees are toxic and which are profitable.

Could this be why there is such a struggle in the Church today? Does this analogy capture the tension that perpetuates your heart and mine? After all, if we're honest, most of us find ourselves caught.

We see unbelievers succulently picking the fruit of culture. Like people shopping a farmer's market, they delicately hold their fruit of choice. They squeeze it and caress it; they roll it over ever so gently in their hands. We see them raise it to their lips and bite into its luscious flesh. They groan over the pleasure the fruit brings to their soul as drops of juice drip down their chin.

We want it. But, we're not sure what fruit will kill, what fruit will bring life, and what fruit God created merely for our pleasure just because He loves us.

So, we'll do one of two things. We'll take on the logic of the separatist and reason that since some fruit in the world is toxic, all fruit must be avoided. We'll gravitate toward a perspective that avoids critical evaluation and thus boycott every type of fruit the world produces.

Or we'll take on the logic of the conformist and say, "Oh, it's not worth the effort. I don't want to expend the energy. It takes too many brain cells to biblically discern what is profitable and what is toxic. Therefore, I'll just consume everything. I'll feed on anything."

The watching world looks on at this behavior and forms two conclusions. Concerning the separatists, the world believes such Christians are out of touch with the real world. They're without joy. They're motivated by law and judging others. They're against everything. Their main motivation is to prevent anyone from enjoying anything. They believe the separatist is narrow-minded and intolerant.

Concerning the conformist, the watching world believes such Christians are no different than themselves. It fails to see any salt or light. The world is turned off by the reality that immorality, lying, and slander characterizes the conformist. In fact, the conformist is usually the one who joins in and verbally crucifies the separatist for his or her legalistic views. The world views the conformist as liberal and tolerant, an exact representation of them.

Thus, both camps, instead of being relevant to their world, become completely irrelevant. Really, I have found that being relevant is reserved for the courageous few. Only a small remnant is willing to take the journey. Most would rather be comfortable than relevant. Most would rather not be in the world at all (separatists) or be completely immersed in the world (conformists).

The separatist justifies himself by claiming allegiance to faith. The conformist justifies himself by claiming allegiance to culture. The few, the transformists, are willing to live on the fine line of embracing faith and culture. As you may have guessed, the concept is simple. The incarnation is another story.

MY JOURNAL IN THE JOURNEY

A God of Gray

June 1998

A young man somewhere between the edge of earth and sea.
That place where sky and heaven converge as one.
That place of you and me.

It used to be so well defined, those boundaries of black and white.
But now it seems as though they've mixed
And I'm standing here asking why?

Part of who I was, defined by what you were.
Now these lines are broken
And so my heart as well.

The fool sees confusion and so he reasons to step foot into the emptiness
below.
At least he's moving,
More than I could ever know.

Some say it will pass.
Only time will tell.
That's nice but what's right for the present moment?

Denial of emotions,
Too often a habit
There's safety within nothing.

Wanting to love,
I see a God of Gray,
And ask for truth to be defined.

But for now I'm content
To be discontent
I'm satisfied with being not.

This God of Gray
In a time as this,
Says trust me by waiting for black and white.

A young man between the edge of earth and sea.
That place when sky and heaven converge as one
That place of you and me.

CHAPTER 2

THE JOURNEY

"THOSE WHO TURN BACK KNOW ONLY THE ORDEAL,
BUT THEY WHO PERSEVERE REMEMBER THE ADVENTURE."
—*Milo L. Arnold*

BY PICKING up this book, you're in the minority. You've taken the first step in a journey. You've exhibited a great amount of courage by even choosing to explore the conversation of how to balance faith with culture. If you're like me, you cringe with fear and excitement when you embark on a new adventure. The anticipation of the unknown threatens to kill you, but at the same time, it's what gets you up in the morning. You detest the routine, the mundane, and the unexamined life. You long to live within the tension.

You want to understand if you have what it takes. You long to breathe the freshness and wonder of life. You desire to know with all your heart if in the very fiber of your being you are relevant. You know this world is not meant to be your final home, but for the time being, it's all you know. You long to live within the balance of being true to both faith and culture without compromising either one. This is your longing, but you're not sure what that even truly means.

You may not have all the answers, but you know that balancing faith with culture has something to do with being relevant. As seen in the figure below, it makes sense on paper, but you're not quite sure how it looks in real life with real people in real settings.

Figure 2.1 - Faith and Culture

You want to be relevant. There is no alternative. Irrelevancy is not an option. When has being obsolete, archaic, or ineffective ever been a viable choice?

Let's be honest though—being relevant is scary. It's not something that is imparted or attained. Like anything of value in this life, it takes hard work and dedication. Relevancy is not for the faint of heart or the intellectual slouch.

Many of us are somewhere in a land of uninvited guests, where neither the world nor the traditional Church seems too appealing. In some ways we're quite thrilled. In other ways we're terrified. There is a nagging reality that something more exists. This can't be all there is. We can't quite put our finger on it, but certainly a relationship with God has to be about more than duty and rules or mindless conformity to culture.

This journey you're about to take will lead you into a fog of tension. It will define the gray and explore the gray. It will take courage to face areas of irrelevancy in your life. It will take even more courage to adjust these areas in order to become relevant.

I've been on this journey for the last several years. I'm closer to relevancy than when I started, but

> **WHEN HAS BEING OBSOLETE, ARCHAIC, OR INEFFECTIVE EVER BEEN A VIABLE CHOICE?**

just like everyone else, I still have a long way to go. It's been a struggle, but the adventure has been unbelievable. As I began on this road, it was like downing a cool, refreshing glass of water on a hot, scorched day. For me, a wandering nomad, traveling through a land called Christianity, it was as if I'd finally found an oasis that quenched a long and overdue thirst.

Let's just say my experience with organized Church had left me wanting. It was good and all, but after attending a Christian elementary and high school, graduating from a Bible institute, a Christian college, and a theological seminary, and now employed as a student ministries pastor, I suppose the wonder of God had somehow fallen by the wayside.

I guess I saw how the "Christian subculture" was making me more and more irrelevant with the people I was trying to interface with. I felt like I was becoming more and more withdrawn from the world. I was convinced I needed to be more relevant, but what did that mean? Was it as simple as getting a couple tattoos (one in Greek and one in Hebrew), a new wardrobe, some edgier music, and some books on philosophy, poetry, and saving the planet? Is this what being relevant means?

After all, the argument on being relevant begs the question, What does it mean to be relevant? If our generation is going to draw a line in the sand against dead orthodoxy and heartless religion, then we better know not only what we are turning from, but also what we are turning to in its place.

I realized several years ago that God was inviting me to join Him on a journey. I had no idea what this journey would bring or where this journey would eventually lead. I was clueless when I started. Now looking back, I couldn't even fathom a glimpse of the abundant life that it would bring. On the same note, I couldn't have predicted how close I came to giving up for good. God used people, circumstances, and pain to bring me to a point where I was completely naked. I'm referring to the type of nakedness that causes you to feel so utterly helpless, exhausted, and hopeless that you barely want to breathe. After He crushed me and drove me into the ground, He breathed new life into me. He set me on the road to relevance.

This road is long. It's difficult. It's paved with blood and tears, laughs and dreams, sweat and toil. The process of becoming relevant isn't easy. After all, when in history has dying ever been easy?

I don't know the specific events God has in store for you. I can't tell you what lies around the bend. One thing I do know is that, like me, you too are plagued with the same irrelevant extremes that have plagued humanity since the beginning of time. You're not immune. God doesn't want you to remain in a state of irrelevance. Too many people visit that place and permanently remain there. God wants you to join Him in a journey that is so incredibly beyond comprehension it's unexplainable. It's a journey that can't be described; it must be experienced. This journey is the incarnation of a transformed mind.

God's intention for you is not that you remain a separatist or a conformist forever. These extremes are safe and uneventful. These are places of apathy. Both these camps have checked out of the journey. These people simply set up shop and dwell in a place of faithless living.

God wants you to follow in the footsteps of His Son, the timeless transformist. He is so passionate, so ridiculously fired up about it, that He actually came in the flesh to model how it can and should be done. If you're not in the journey on the road to relevance, then you are not in the game.

GETTING IN THE GAME

Let's start here. What does the word "relevant" mean to you? What emotions or feelings does it evoke? Skepticism? Excitement? Cynicism? Confusion? Longing? This trendy word "relevant" means so many things to so many people. Some see it as something to be sought after. Others see it as a term that labels someone who has denied the faith.

Recently I sat down with a dean of a seminary here in the Midwest. He explained how the seminary was shifting its focus and streamlining its effectiveness. A major point in this process was to come up with five core values that represent the seminary's intent. One of the five core values that surfaced is to be culturally relevant.

Does this seminary have a plan to bring about relevance? Do they have a road map or course of action to attain relevancy? More importantly, do they have a standard of measurement to track their relevancy? After all, if we are fuzzy in our definition, we will be fuzzy in our destination. We are intentionally fuzzy when it comes to being relevant, because relevance itself is fuzzy.

Is this our best attempt? Do we just shrug our shoulders and say, "Well, I hope to be relevant with my faith and the culture around, but I'm not really sure how to get there, or even what it means"?

The first step on the road to relevancy is to demystify what it means. Webster defines relevant as "having significant and demonstrable bearing on the matter at hand; appropriateness to the subject."[1] Synonyms for relevant are: germane, pertinent, and applicable.

Shouldn't Christianity be significant? Shouldn't we have demonstrable bearing within our world? Shouldn't the Church have a pertinent effect in these times we find ourselves in?

We must understand that being relevant has nothing inherently to do with the external. This is fundamental, and it must be grasped. I'm not saying that being relevant is all theoretical or abstract. It is incarnational. It must be incarnational in order to be authentic.[2] However, this is not the starting point. In fact, the external is merely the result of the internal conception that takes place beforehand.

In other words, it's not the earrings we wear or the music we listen to that makes us relevant. It's not how close we can come to the line of "mainstream" before we fall into sin. Being relevant is not about the fashion of our vocabulary, the packaging of our philosophical bent, or the level at which we detest the traditional Evangelical Church. These things all breathe of the external.

Relevance is fundamentally internal. It's conceived through an internal relationship with God. Not only is it birthed internally, but it's maintained and sustained from an internal soul directed and connected to the person of Jesus Christ. All of life can and should be the outflow of that relationship. Simply, what makes us relevant is our love for God and people.

God Lover   **People Lover**

RELEVANT

Figure 2.2 - God lover/ People lover

ALL APOLOGIES?

In my flesh, I wish being relevant could be attained another way. It would be so much easier. It would be so much cleaner. Too bad it's not. The first step in being more relevant to my neighbor is not to buy a boat because he likes boating. It's not to become a fan of atheistic literature in order to relate more with the professors down on campus. While these both may pertain somewhat to being relevant, just buying the boat would be missing the boat.

It's not what you do, what you say, what you know, or what you give, that makes you relevant with your faith and culture.

It's not about being trendy or current. There is a language that cuts beyond music, movies, and media. The true language of being relevant is love.

You can't fake it. You can't manufacture it. You can't manipulate it. You can't produce it. Love is timeless. Love is not bound by geography, economy, or philosophy. It transcends all things.

To say, "being relevant means having love," may sound trite or oversimplified. It may conjure up feelings of sappy love songs or juvenile wishful thinking. But wait, let's remember Jesus' reply to the expert in the Mosaic Law who asked Him, "Teacher, which is the greatest commandment in the Law?" Jesus replied:

> *"You shall love the LORD your God with all your heart, and with all your soul, and with all your mind." The second is like it, "You shall love your neighbor as yourself." On these two commandments depend the whole Law and the Prophets. —Matthew 22:35-40*

Think for a second about the most relevant people in the Bible. Their lives were all characterized by love. Let me remind you of a very convicting story Jesus told.

GET OFF YOUR DONKEY

> *A certain man was going down from Jerusalem to Jericho; and he fell among robbers, and they stripped him and beat him, and went off leaving him half dead. And by chance a certain priest was going down on that road, and when he saw him, he passed by on the other side. And likewise a Levite also, when he came to the place and saw him, passed by on the other side. But a certain Samaritan, who was on a journey, came upon him; and when he saw him, he felt compassion, and came to him, and bandaged up his wounds, pouring oil and wine on them; and he put him on his own beast, and brought him to an inn, and took care of him. And on the next day he took out two denarii and gave them to the innkeeper and said, "Take care of him; and whatever more you spend, when I return, I will repay you."*
> *—Luke 10:30-35*

If you were to ask the Jew, who fell among robbers on the road to Jericho, "Who was the most relevant person to you?" What would he say? Was it the priest who knew the Scriptures and current debates of his day? Was it the Levite who was employed in the temple? No. He would say the most relevant person in his life was the Good Samaritan. The relevant man was the one who stopped his busy schedule, pulled over, got off his donkey, cleansed his wounds, cared for him through the night, and paid his medical bills. This Samaritan, the social outcast and irrelevant man of the day, became totally relevant when he displayed love.[3]

The Jew infringed upon the Samaritan's time, tasks, and financial resources. The Samaritan stopped everything in order to be inconvenienced by someone who would traditionally hate him, a Jew. This relevant man chose to get involved.

His clothes could have been bloodied. Quite possibly he even tore them to make bandages. Besides taking the Jew to an inn, the Good Samaritan took care of him through the night. The next day, he told the innkeeper to record all the costs the Jew imposed on him. The Samaritan didn't put a cap on the costs. Rather, he told the innkeeper he'd repay him whatever the costs would be.

In the story, the Good Samaritan was headed somewhere. He had a task. He had a destination. He was traveling. We learn from the passage that his mode of transportation was a beast, possibly a donkey. His donkey represented the ability of reaching his intended destination. Ironically, he got off of it, putting his task on hold, and became relevant to someone who needed love.

Today, many of us are headed somewhere. We have a task, an agenda, a destination. We dare not let anyone inconvenience us on our journey to reach that destination. Our donkey represents the mode of transportation that allows us to reach our goal. Unfortunately, we stay seated on our donkey and pass right by the needs of hurting people.

Where are you headed? What is your dream? What is your destination? Will you sit on your donkey and pass by? Will you justify your apathy because you, like the priest, need to fulfill your godly duties first? Remember, loving people is our godly duty!

The sad thing is for others of us, we're not traveling to any destination. Instead of riding our donkey, we're just sitting on it! We simply take up God's air and God's food and amuse ourselves to death. A wounded world, longing for authentic God lovers and people lovers, awaits you and I to get off our donkey and bandage its wounds in the power of Jesus Christ.

IS IT ANY WONDER THAT LOVE IS THE LANGUAGE OF RELEVANCE?

THE RELEVANT REMNANT

The Scriptures are rich with men and women who became relevant to their world the moment they showed love. Is it any wonder that love is the language of relevance? Think about Christ for a moment. What made the Son of God relevant to a world that knew Him not? It was His love for you and I that transcended culture, space, time, race, and every other boundary humanity tried to throw in His face.

Loving God and loving people sounds too easy. It's too simple. It's not edgy enough. Perhaps all these are true because we have not been taught what loving God with all our heart, soul, and mind, and loving our neighbor as ourselves means. Maybe it's much more profound than we give it credit for being.

My journey has led me on quite a detour. I've traveled through many doors of introspection and evaluation. I've contemplated issues of the clothes I wear, the art I appreciate, and the entertainment I examine, hoping to find the key to relevance. I've longed for that one book or that chosen CD that would impart relevance. It would have been so easy if I'd stumbled upon such a treasure.

God "unfortunately" has led me back, full circle, to a truth I'm only beginning to meander down. It's much more intensive. It's much more dangerous. It's just plain tough. It's a daily ritual of dying to self in order to love my neighbor. It's about loving God and loving people.

The journey toward a transformed mind is only reached through one road. That road, the road to relevance, is loving God and loving people. The truth is that each individual who dares to take the journey will walk a road that looks a little different from everybody else. No road looks exactly the same, because no one is exactly the same. This is what makes the journey so exciting.

No one has walked your specific road before. There is no exact map that prepares you for all the curves and bends God has planned for you. As you move from your irrelevant extremes of separatism and conformity, you will face opposition, heartache, and victory. This is where the adventure lies.

My journey towards relevance has been about rejecting the regiment of religion and the pleas of dead orthodoxy. It's been about a return to the simplistic, yet transformational message of Jesus. It's been about a departure from sacrifice and an embrace toward mercy. But most of all, it's been about love. Do I love God and the people around me? This is the secret of relevancy. Most everything else is irrelevant.

> *Since you have in obedience to the truth purified your souls for a sincere*
> *love of the brethren, fervently love one another*
> *from the heart.*
> *—1 Peter 1:22*

MY JOURNAL IN THE JOURNEY

Need.

April 2000

Cliffs on each side of me, a teeter-totter in the
middle of me. I've been on one extreme my whole
life. Safety is seen in familiarity, even though it
sucks the joy right out of me. That edge. So risky.
So intriguing. It cries out struggle and thus need.
It echoes grace and pictures God. How I've run
my whole life from that teeter-totter of reality. I've
retreated to plateaus that require my own blood.
Emptiness suppressed in absolutes. Legalism. That
friendly system that demands my devotion.
Heartless choices and human devices require
the mystery of my relationship with Him.

Didn't know my Lord, 'cause I never had to trust.
Sanctification is carved in do's and don'ts.
Can't give anything to anyone because I've never
quite grasped it myself. The day I dared to get up
on that teeter-totter I told myself it was safer in
my hell. These days I'm getting more bruised than
ever. But I've learned that by embracing the struggle
I've found the Savior and realized He's been patiently
waiting there all along.

CHAPTER 3

THE PARADIGM

HELEN KELLER WAS ASKED, "DO YOU KNOW OF ANYTHING THAT'S WORSE THAN BEING BLIND?" SHE THOUGHT FOR A MOMENT AND THEN SAID, "YES, THERE IS ONE THING WORSE THAN BEING BLIND—HAVING SIGHT WITH NO VISION."

I NEVER enjoyed jigsaw puzzles. Call me uncreative or impatient, I just preferred climbing trees or building forts. To this day I prefer a trip to the dentist rather than wrestling with assembling a five thousand-piece jigsaw puzzle.

23

Why do I have a thing against puzzles? What did they ever do to me? I guess I just like to see a completed picture. When I examine the individual puzzle pieces, I become confused and frustrated. I fail to understand the part each piece plays in the overall scheme of things. It's only when the picture is complete that I appreciate the many pieces that together make up the whole.

In this chapter, we're going to examine a new paradigm. It's a whole different way of thinking and interfacing with the world around us. There are several components that play a significant role. These components are like puzzle pieces that make sense when assembled with the larger paradigm. I want to first look at the completed picture before we examine the individual pieces. Then, for the next several chapters, we'll take an in-depth look at the specific components making up this paradigm.

Please hear me out—this chapter is fairly comprehensive. Take your time as you critically wade through some of the new language introduced. Remember, we're on a journey, not in a race. Enjoy the process.

THE TRANSFORMED MIND

Any new way of thinking requires a paradigm shift. There is no exception when dialoguing about balancing faith and culture with loving God and people. Our paradigm, called the Transformed Mind Paradigm, is pictured below.

Figure 3.1 - The Transformed Mind Paradigm

If we aim to complete the puzzle of relevancy, three crucial factors must be kept in the forefront of our minds.

#1 Integration
#2 Incarnation
#3 Balance

IT'S ALL ABOUT INTEGRATION

First, we must integrate. There is no possible way to determine from our paradigm where loving God begins and where loving people stops. This is intentional. The Bible explains that we can't have one without the other. We can't love God and hate our brother.

> *If someone says, "I love God," and hates his brother, he is a liar; for the one who does not love his brother whom he has seen, cannot love God whom he has not seen.*
> *—1 John 4:20*

The opposite is true as well. We can't fully love our brother and hate God. It's impossible to fully love our brother and hate the God in whose image we're all created. Besides, God is love. Love is from God, and in God love dwells.

> *Beloved, let us love one another, for love is from God; and everyone who loves is born of God and knows God. The one who does not love does not know God, for God is love.*
> *—1 John 4:7-8*

In other words, loving God and loving people are interconnected. They must intersect, because they're inherently integrated in all facets. They can't be extracted from each other because they're two sides of the same coin. They're linked. You can't have one without the other.

Likewise, as seen in our paradigm, you can't determine where faith starts and culture stops. You cannot distinguish how these two components are distinct from each other. They bleed over and spill into one another. They too are blended and interfaced.

Many people's lives do not reflect this integration quality. They attempt to separate their love for God from their love for people. Many see their faith and their culture as two completely distinct entities that never should mix. Usually this means one of two things: Either they have no clue how to integrate their faith with their culture, or they are deathly afraid of what it might mean if they tried. Both the separatist and the conformist fail to integrate.

Separatists have their Christian friends, their Christian music, and their Christian church. They wear their faith all the time, but fail to relate with the world around them. They pride themselves in having a pure faith. Separatists fail to see that no one wants to hear about their faith, because they're completely irrelevant to the culture all around. When you challenge them to integrate their faith with their culture, they get a frightened look in their eyes. They don't want to integrate because what you're asking them to do essentially is to release control.

Conformists propose to live a one-day religion. For those who even go to church on Sunday for about two hours, they look, act, and speak like someone who follows Christ. However, after hitting the exit door, they immediately place their faith on the shelf and live the rest of their week completely conformed to culture. Additionally, they fragment their faith from their culture. In fact, many conformists are so polished at this that they can temporarily wear their faith and take it off at will. They can display their faith when it's convenient and remove it when it proves to be uncomfortable.

These cases illustrate individuals who swing to one irrelevant extreme or the other. Such people fail to understand that faith, culture, love for God, and love for people can't be categorized or segmented from the other necessary and interdependent components. People who fail to integrate fail to fit with our paradigm. If a man desires to be a transformist, he will practically integrate his faith with his culture and his love for God with his love for people.

THE EDGE OF INCARNATION

According to the Transformed Mind Paradigm, the second factor we must understand is the vital need for it to be applied in real life. It's very easy to write a book about how to balance faith with culture. It's a whole different matter to live a life that balances faith with culture.

If we're going to experience a paradigm shift, we need to reintroduce a curious word. Most of us have heard the term

> **RELEVANCE IS THE UNAVOIDABLE BY-PRODUCT OF A REAL LIVE PERSON LOVING GOD AND LOVING PEOPLE.**

"incarnation."[1] It's a word given to us by theologians that describes the process of Jesus' coming to the earth as a man. John clearly describes the incarnation when he writes, "And the Word became flesh, and dwelt among us."[2] In street language, although perhaps oversimplified, the incarnation refers to God with skin on.

This is a beautiful picture that relates to our paradigm. In other words, for our paradigm to transform culture, it must be "fleshed out" in the life of an individual. The Transformed Mind Paradigm is incomplete until it is lived out. Our paradigm must have skin on it. It can't exist without being incarnated into the life of a transformist.

Without incarnation, we are just theorists. Without our paradigm infused into the life of a real person with a set of real issues, we are only speculating. What makes the paradigm relevant, what gives it life, is the edge of incarnation.

Look back to figure 3.1. Notice the teeter-totter is balanced upon a fulcrum. Without this fulcrum, our paradigm is simply a flat board. It's lifeless. It's merely another philosophical model. This is the reality when we fail to incarnate our paradigm.

The fulcrum represents something significant. It symbolizes life. This pivotal point illustrates a real person with a real set of issues. It pictures the threshold where theory meets practicality, where knowing the path confronts walking the path.[3] This is the edge of incarnation.

The fulcrum, symbolizing the life of an individual, forces the paradigm to move from the written page into everyday life. Incarnation prevents the paradigm from evolving into a place of irrelevance. Relevance is the unavoidable by-product of a real live person loving God and loving people.

BALANCING BALANCE

The third and final factor we must come to grips with is the vital need for balance. Hopefully you're beginning to see that a balanced life is a relevant life. The transformist is the individual who balances faith and culture with loving God and people. Looking at our paradigm, we can see that the teeter-totter is balanced. This is key!

But what is balance? Is it a plan or pattern? Is it a program or set of rules we post on the wall? More importantly, what brings balance? Perhaps the theologically accurate question is who brings balance?

> *For the grace of God has appeared, bringing salvation to all men, instructing us*
> *to deny ungodliness and worldly desires and to live sensibly,*
> *righteously and godly in the present age.*
> *—Titus 2:11-12*

Notice that this passage refers to the incarnation of Jesus. The grace of God that appeared, bringing salvation to all men, took place when the Son of God came in the flesh as a man.[4] Jesus Christ is the literal manifestation of God's grace. It is Jesus who instructs us how to deny ungodliness and unhealthy desires.[5] In other words, Jesus teaches us how to say "no" to certain things.[6]

Likewise, it is Jesus who teaches us how to say "yes" to living sensibly, righteously, and godly in the present age.[7] This English word "sensibly" will be our focus for the time being. Providentially, I'm very familiar with this word, although originally not by choice.

Several years ago, for my exegetical in Greek class, I was randomly assigned Titus 2:11-15. Little did I know, God was planning to use (of all things) a word study on "sensibly" to convict me of my separatist tendencies.

At this time in my life, I was using lists, rules, and religion to control my relationship with culture—or lack thereof. I was attempting to live a life of holiness based on legalism. I labeled all activities in life as sacred or secular in an attempt to minimize the gray.

Initially I was not too thrilled spending eight hours researching the obscure Greek word *sophronos* and its usage throughout historical literature. However, like so many times before, God had other things in mind. He used this passage to reveal the intense fear and control I exhibited in my walk of "faith." I had trusted in personal rules for every aspect in my life, including the movies I watched, the books I read, the people I hung out with, and the music I listened to.

What I didn't realize was that my life was completely unbalanced. In my zeal for God and personal holiness, I had become irrelevant to people and the world around me. I had prided myself in attaining a pure faith, but I was blinded to sin that popped up in so many other areas of my life. I needed balance. I knew that much.

Through this word study, God showed me it's through Christ and within Christ that I have any hope of living a balanced life. No amount of rules, man-made religion, or programs will teach me balance. No human plan can curb, control, or implement balanced living.

NO HUMAN PLAN CAN CURB, CONTROL, OR IMPLEMENT BALANCED LIVING.

Sophronos means to be self-controlled, temperate, or moderate. Many times it's translated sober. Think for a second. What characterizes someone who is not sober? Without a doubt, it's unbalance. People who are drunk can't walk, much less stand. They're completely unbalanced.

Surprisingly, Titus 2:11-12 is literally saying that Christ will teach me how live a balanced life. It reads, "For the grace of God has appeared, (*through the person of Jesus Christ*) ... instructing us to live ... sensibly (*balanced*) in the present age." [italicized phrases mine].[8]

This truth came as a wake-up call. God showed me the secret to balanced living. It was within His Son. Coming from a past steeped in legalism, I'd been defeated time and time again by an emphasis on laws and rules as a means of balanced, self-controlled, and godly living. Like most separatists, inside my heart resided the Pharisee who cried out for liberation from slavery to rules and religion. I learned that it was for freedom that Christ set me free.[9] It's Christ who teaches me how to maintain balance.

Likewise, conformists can find true freedom in Christ. They no longer have to settle for an "anything goes" philosophy of life. Many conformists, for fear of irrelevance and boredom, settle for a lifestyle that thoughtlessly consumes culture. They too can transform culture through a balanced life.

Examining the life of Christ, we see tremendous balance. He had communion with the Father and ministry with the multitudes.[10] He had meals with Mary and Martha and debates with the teachers of the law.[11] He raised the dead and at times retreated from those who needed healing.[12]

I learned through this word study in Greek class that as I am whipped back and forth between the extremes of being a separatist or conformist, legalism and license, it's only within Christ that I'll find a balanced life. No longer do I need to seek outside of what God has provided for a sanctified life. It's through Him and in Him that I have balance in my daily living.

Jesus not only modeled a balanced life, but He also commanded a balanced life. In fact, He mandated a balanced life for His disciples.

> *Behold, I send you out as sheep in the midst of wolves;*
> *therefore be shrewd as serpents, and innocent as doves.*
> *—Matthew 10:16*

The Bible records many real life examples of men and women who became unbalanced in their living.[13] The Pharisees made religious works their goal and missed the mark. Solomon made pleasure his goal and came to ruin. Both works and pleasure are good, but both must be in balance with the Word of God.

> *Do not be excessively righteous, and do not be overly wise.*
> *Why should you ruin yourself? Do not be excessively wicked, and do not be a fool.*
> *Why should you die before your time?*
> *—Ecclesiastes 3:16-17*

As you think back to the paradigm, notice the fulcrum forces our model out of a static position. As a result, because circumstances in us are constantly changing, the paradigm is constantly changing. It moves because we move. Without fail, as situations come up every day in our lives, we are forced to balance the teeter-totter. We never reach a plateau where we have fully mastered how to balance faith with culture.

Although we may reach a point where, through our personal relationship with God, we can steadily maintain balance, we'll never be able to reach a permanent place of balance. God doesn't want us to. He wants us to struggle, because it's within the struggle that we learn dependence on Him.

A WORD FROM THE CHESHIRE CAT[14]

Alice came to crossroads. She spied the Cheshire Cat in a nearby tree. "Which road should I take?" she asked the cat.

"Where do you want to get to?" the cat asked helpfully.

"I don't know," she admitted.

"Then," advised the cat, "any road will take you there."

Today, many followers of Jesus are in the exact same predicament as Alice. This scenario is reenacted time and time again. We are just not quite sure where we are headed. Thus, any road will be the right one.

Most of us wander throughout culture. We don't have a plan. We certainly are without a map. We are meandering carelessly down whatever path strikes our fancy. The watching world sees us pilgrims as irrelevant and aimless—not quite what they'd want to model themselves after.

This chapter has offered you, the sojourner, a compass for your journey. It has identified the road to relevance. It has diagrammed the destination. But is it right? Will it work? If doesn't work, what causes it to fail?

The road is right because it's simply made up of the greatest two commandments, to love God and love people.[15] It will work because it has worked. The Scriptures are full of relevant people who balanced faith and culture with loving God and people.

The paradigm fails when we fail to integrate, incarnate, and remain balanced. When we gravitate toward irrelevant extremes, which will always be our fleshly tendency, we become unbalanced and jeopardize our relevance.

Are you ready to move beyond the theoretical? Do you want to continue on the journey? Perhaps we should look in the mirror at our own irrelevant extremes. This very well might be the scariest part of the journey yet—the journey inside oneself.

Test yourselves to see if you are in the faith; examine yourselves! Or do you not recognize this about yourselves, that Jesus Christ is in you—unless indeed you fail the test?
—2 Corinthians 13:5

Let us examine and probe our ways, And let us return to the LORD.
—Lamentations 3:40

MY JOURNAL IN THE JOURNEY

The Box
October 1999

Bound by walls, I find myself within a box
Never asked for such a prison, it's just always been
After years of intimacy, I guess it's a part of me
Once a friend, now it leaves me broken and restricted

I guess it's easy to get used to perpetual rape
From the outside, people tell me to just walk away
How am I supposed to know if this isn't just truth
With lines of light and darkness, where does origin begin

Do they blend or is the box well defined
Who is the authority, the heart or the mind
Both whisper words of advice and I'm just here
Getting used by my box that seems so cordial

Better to be a slave than to be alone and free
At least my enemies now take the form of flesh
This box has beauty even though it's abuse
Just don't stop killing me, I couldn't deal with that

I guess it's leaving me with a piece of insanity
It's just too unsafe to let go of the box
The world would be just too gray for me to deal with
At least my enemies now take the form of flesh

CHAPTER 4=
THE SEPARATISTS

"MOST PEOPLE DIE WITH THEIR MUSIC STILL INSIDE THEM."
—*Oliver Wendell Holmes*

I LOVED going to Grandma Millie's house up north. Besides the fact that we took a retreat from the city, I could always count on her treasured candy bowl residing on the coffee table. My parents were much too wise to leave cinnamon bears and caramels lying around unattended at our house.

But this was Grandma Millie's house, and she thought differently.

After I took the initial dive into the candy bowl, she would always tell me, "Kary, remember to have balance. Too much of anything will make you sick." Several times while laying sprawled out on the couch (after taking some Pepto Bismol for my stomachache), I found myself vowing next time to follow Grandma's advice about balance.

Balance in the spiritual world is no different. Irrelevancy creeps into the door of the heart when a Christian becomes unbalanced. We get sick and placed upon the couch of irrelevancy when we forget to keep Jesus' message of loving God and loving people in balance.

When we become unbalanced in loving God and loving people, we swing to one of two extremes. If we "love" God in absence of loving people, we become separatists. If we "love" people in absence of loving God, we become conformists.

I have found myself many times spiritually sick and laying on the couch of irrelevancy because I have done just that. I have been a separatist, and I have been a conformist. The Church is no different. In fact, at times, I've seen her lying next to me on the couch with the same sick look in her eye.

For many of us, if we're really honest, when we look into the mirror that reflects our spiritual condition, we find ourselves looking a lot like separatists. We're bound with fear. We're consumed with control. We, like the Pharisees of old, make rules and regulations in an attempt to create, control, and curb personal holiness. The Pharisees for fear of breaking The Ten Commandments, made 613 additional laws, 365 which were negative (thou shall not) and 248 which were positive (thou shall).[1] Some of us have made more. Some of us have made less. In any case, many of us are bound and enslaved, rather than free and liberated.

Ironically, Jesus came that you and I might have life and have it abundantly.[2] How many followers of Jesus do you know are living the abundant life? So many believers put on Jesus only to get a ticket out of hell. If His main purpose was to give us abundant life, then why is there so much joyless, man-made religiosity? In our pursuit of holiness, have most of us just been washed up on the irrelevant shores of separatism?

CIRCLES OF SEPARATISM

Whereas the motives of a separatist may seem pure, the outcome is outright heretical. Many separatists add to God's commands in an attempt to prevent sin. In Jesus' time, the Pharisees created many ridiculous laws. In fact, Jesus was not amused when exposed to those rules. Instead of being impressed by the weighty man-made laws, the Son of God was downright appalled.

And they tie up heavy loads, and lay them on men's shoulders; but they themselves are unwilling to move them with so much as a finger ... Woe to you, scribes and Pharisees, hypocrites! For you tithe mint and dill and cummin, and have neglected the weightier provisions of the law: justice and mercy and faithfulness; but these are the things you should have done without neglecting the others.
—Matthew 23:4,23

Obviously there is much to be said about a Christian's attitudes toward alcohol.[3] This is an important discussion. There are laws that must be observed both legally and biblically. Irresponsible alcohol use has damaged many people's lives. However, for the sake of our discussion, I want to briefly highlight one practical example how many separatists add to God's law.

The Bible is clear that being drunk is wrong. Also, an addiction to alcohol excludes a man from serving as an elder or deacon in the Church.[4] However, in order to not infringe upon this standard, many of us add concentric circles of separatism that distance us from alcohol. This is completely acceptable if it's a personal God-given conviction.

Two problems come into the picture very rapidly if we're not too careful. First, our personal convictions can soon be viewed (to us personally or to those around us) as on the same level of biblical standards. This is not only dangerous, but it's also heresy. Secondly, we can begin to separate ourselves from people who drink. This is a practice that is completely offensive to God. We are not told to separate ourselves from people who drink, much less those who struggle with the really "big sins."

I wrote you in my letter not to associate with immoral people; I did not at all mean with the immoral people of this world, or with the covetous and swindlers, or with idolaters, for then you would have to go out of the world.
—*1 Corinthians 5:9-10*

What circles of separatism have you erected in your own life? Are your convictions God-given or adaptations of another person's convictions? Do you view your personal convictions as on the same level as God's Word? Do you judge others with your set of rules?

DECEIVED GOD LOVERS

Referring back to our paradigm, let's take a look at how separatists' faith and culture are unbalanced from their love for God and people.

In their pursuit of holiness, separatists justify themselves as God lovers, deceive themselves, and often become an offense to people. You can spot a separatist a mile a way. They claim to love people, but their "strong" stance for purity and truth alienates them from people and God. They are completely irrelevant.

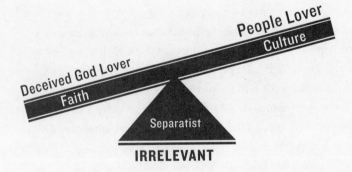

Figure 4.1 - The Irrelevant Separatist

Notice Jesus found the Pharisees both repulsive and detrimental. He knew these were the people whose hearts were the most spiritually sick. After all, they were extremely unhealthy and didn't even know it.

So where do separatists get fuel for their fire? Interestingly enough, they pick random verses out of context while failing to examine the whole of Scripture. They approach the Bible with a preconceived grid that allows them to see what they want to see.[5] They cling to these verses as proof that God wants them to retreat from culture. In fact, many believe with all their hearts that they're God lovers. Below is some of the often-used ammo in the arsenal of the separatist.

*You adulteresses, do you not know
that friendship with the world is hostility toward God? Therefore whoever
wishes to be a friend of the world makes himself an enemy of God.*
—James 4:4

*This is pure and undefiled religion in the sight of our God and Father,
to visit orphans and widows in their distress, and to keep oneself unstained by the world.*
—James 1:27

*Beloved, I urge you as aliens and strangers to abstain from fleshly lusts,
which wage war against the soul.*
—1 Peter 2:11

*I have given them Thy word; and the world has hated them,
because they are not of the world, even as I am not of the world. I do not ask Thee to take
them out of the world, but to keep them from the evil one. They are not of the world,
even as I am not of the world. Sanctify them in the truth; Thy word is truth. As Thou
didst send Me into the world, I also have sent them into the world.*
—John 17:14-18

*... who gave Himself for our sins, that He might deliver
us out of this present evil age, according to the will of our God and Father ...*
—Galatians 1:4

The god of this age has blinded the minds of unbelievers,
so that they cannot see the light of the gospel of
the glory of Christ, who is the image of God.
—2 Corinthians 4:4 (NIV)

And if anyone does not obey our instruction in this letter,
take special note of that man and do not associate with him,
so that he may be put to shame.
—2 Thessalonians 3:14

Do not love the world, nor the things in the world.
If anyone loves the world, the love of the Father is not in him.
For all that is in the world, the lust of the flesh and the lust of
the eyes and the boastful pride of life, is not from the Father,
but is from the world. And the world is passing away,
and also its lusts; but the one who does the will of God abides forever.
—1 John 2:15-17

"Therefore, come out from their midst and be separate," says the Lord.
"And do not touch what is unclean; And I will welcome you."
—2 Corinthians 6:17

MIRROR, MIRROR ON THE WALL

Separatism runs so deep. How do we unwrap the many layers that characterize this irrelevant extreme? For starters, let's examine ourselves in the mirror that reflects our spiritual condition and see how we look.

Many components contribute to someone being characterized as one who struggles with separatism. However, when we look at a separatist, often three common traits rise to the surface. A separatist allows 1) rules to replace relationships, 2) microscopes to replace mirrors, and 3) performance to replace passion.

How do you look? Do you struggle with any of these? Do you allow rules, rather than your relationship with God, to dictate your diet of culture? Do you find yourself constantly judging others for their personal choices, rather than examining your own heart? Do you feel driven by duty and performance, rather than by authentic devotion and passion?

If any of these are remotely true about you, then you probably struggle with tendencies of separatism. If you look pretty good when you examine yourself in the mirror of separatism, just wait. In the next chapter, we'll look into the mirror of conformity. I have found in my own life, at different times concerning different issues, I struggle with both the tendencies of a separatist and a conformist, sometimes even in the same day. Maybe you will find the same to be true.

Even if you're a conformist, reading this chapter will allow you to understand the thought process behind the separatist. This is the first step toward the healing process that must take place within our current Church age.

If you're a separatist, take this chapter at a slow pace. The examples given are intentionally extreme. I've done this in order to demonstrate the incorrect thinking patterns and courses of actions that characterize the separatist. Remember, this part of the journey may be difficult. After all, when has looking into the mirror ever been easy?

CATEGORY CREATORS

A separatist is one who lives life in fear. They set up fortresses away from society and hide within them. They categorize all art, music, philosophy, and entertainment as either being sacred or secular. There is no middle ground.

For the separatist, activities such as drinking coffee, exercising, reading, shopping, or cleaning must be justified by slapping the name of Jesus upon it. The worldly becomes spiritual only when it is placed within the category of Christian. All other activities pose a subtle attack that threatens to erode away one's sanctification and personal holiness.

Just categorizing activities isn't enough, and soon separatists begin categorizing people. Now the Christian is limited not only by activities, but also by environment. The separatist can't sanctify (make holy) culture, and so he retreats from it. He thinks life is all about suffering for the name of Christ and being persecuted for radical stances against culture. Separatists are self-proclaimed martyrs. They create a subculture filled with Christian books, Christian music, Christian clothes, and Christian stores.

They boast of their love for God and use that as fuel for their "suffering." It's because separatists love God that they attend church every time the doors are open. In fact, the Church is really a safe haven to get away from the heathen reprobates in the world. Loving people means boycotting the world only some of the time and especially on Sundays.

Separatists often try to sanctify things God never labeled as unholy. Not all music, exercise, movies, media, art, and learning are unholy. Yet separatists try to "Christianize" them. Dan Buck, in his article, "Getting Out of the Faith Ghetto," asserted:

> The problem is categories. We have categorized ourselves out of the world. Life is one category. Good music, good art, good health, and good prescription drugs are innately spiritual if they are in fact good. We don't need to label something Christian to the exclusion of the rest of the world for it to be good and pure, because all things that are good and pure are of God. All truth is God's truth. If we are seeking God out of everything we do, He will inevitably show up. He doesn't need labels or categories to find us, and we shouldn't need them to find Him. Sure, there are experiences that we should stay away from, but He has given us a mind, the Holy Spirit, and a body of believers to help us decipher what is of Him and what is not. Our categories have become the lazy Christian's guide to prudence. Truth. It is not supposed to be easy. Every experience, every person you meet and every choice you make is part of the walk.[6]

Look at some of the ridiculous categories we create. No longer do we drink coffee just to drink coffee. Now we have Christian coffee shops. It's as if slapping the name of Jesus on coffee will sanctify (the caffeine out of) it.

There are now Christian vitamin companies and Christian workout clubs. At face value, this may seem innocent or tolerable. However, as we unwrap the ramifications behind such companies and clubs, we'll see the dangers far outweigh the benefits.

Paul acknowledges the profit of bodily exercise.[7] I don't know any pastor who would tell his church family to trash their bodies. In fact, Scriptures tell us our bodies are the temple of the Holy Spirit.[8] Therefore, taking care of our bodies, whether in the form of vitamins or exercising, is biblical.

However, when we slap the name of Jesus on taking care of our bodies, we unnecessarily confuse the watching world. Also, in our attempt to be holy, like good separatists always do, we break

> OUR MISSION IS NOT TO BUILD A CHRISTIAN SUBCULTURE. IT'S NOT TO SANCTIFY OUR CULTURE EITHER.

several of God's other commands that we will look at in a moment. For now, remember Paul's directive to the Corinthian Church about avoiding separatism.

> *I wrote you in my letter not to associate with immoral people; I did not at all mean with the immoral people of this world, or with the covetous and swindlers, or with idolaters; for then you would have to go out of the world.*
> *—2 Corinthians 5:9-10*

The reality is that separatists have attempted to leave the world. They can't fulfill the Great Commission because they're not willing to go into all the world.[9] Just like the architects of the Tower of Babel, separatists want to create, congregate, and build a name for themselves.

Do I sound harsh? I'm not sitting on my hobbyhorse condemning and judging. If I'm honest, I'd admit that my dream is to walk around in a monk's robe writing, reading, and making "important" theological discoveries.

God wants so much more for us separatists. God has always been

43

about spreading His godly seed throughout the world. Catch this. God's first mission for His chosen ones, Adam and Eve, was to fill the earth with righteous people.[10] God's last command to His chosen ones, the Church, is to fill the earth with righteous disciples.[11]

Our mission is not to build a Christian subculture. It's not to sanctify our culture either. Our mission is to make disciples of all nations, teaching them to observe all Christ commanded. In that mission, God may choose to sanctify culture, but that's His prerogative.

DOESN'T MATTER IF YOU'RE BLACK OR WHITE

Many separatists believe it's not a good idea to consume anything the world produces. The risk is too great, the temptation too strong. Since some of the art, literature, philosophy, music, media, science, and psychology produced by the "secular" world is bad, none of it is good. This is not only damaging, but (as we'll soon examine in detail) it's bad theology as well. It's unbalanced. While there is a world system set against the purposes and principles of God, not everything the world produces is bad. Nonetheless, separatists create categories for everything. Nothing is gray. Everything is black and white.

A black and white mindset breeds safety. It allows the separatist to attain his most coveted characteristic—CONTROL! Gray is too slippery. It's too dangerous. It must be weeded out and replaced with black or white.

To admit that some of the world contains gray would be to admit that not everything can be managed. To admit that not everything can be managed would be to forfeit control. When everything is black and white, things make sense and can be controlled. The separatist is in a position of power, rather than a position of dependence.

When a "gray" activity arises within the world, two options arise. The first option is to avoid the activity. To engage in the activity would mean to compromise and become stained. The second option is to create a Christian alternative that sanctifies the activity.

Interestingly enough, sometimes the Christian alternative is not created to combat a sinful activity owned by the world. Rather, the alternative simply justifies or spiritualizes the previously neutral activity. After all, if something is neutral, it must be redeemed for the sake of the kingdom. It must bear the name of Jesus.

As a result, we now have Christian candy, Christian coffee shops, Christian T-shirts, Christian music, Christian phone books that list Christian businesses, and even Jesus action figures. The Christian market is an industry that creates billions of dollars every year. The world is not stupid. They're jumping on the bandwagon to get their piece of the pie.

Kenneth L. Woodward, *Newsweek*'s chief religion writer, has a fairly accurate picture of the market: "I'll tell you what sells. It's been true for at least twenty-five years. Religion covers are always the first, second, and third best-selling covers on the newsstand for *Time* and *Newsweek*. It's mostly Jesus who sells. For a while the pope sold, but the pope's too old and doesn't sell now. 'God and the Brain' sold, but mostly it's Jesus."[12]

Am I against the Christian market? I believe there's tremendous good coming from much of the market. Some artists are passionate about using their God-given talents to promote the Gospel. They serve a fantastic purpose of orienting our thoughts, emotions, and spirits to worshiping God. Quality music, drama, art, and books are being produced, some of them very thought provoking. However, what's the standard of measurement that determines our success of meeting our Master's mission?

A FALSE SENSE OF VICTORY?

Several months back, I was watching a special report about the homosexual movement. It expressed the tremendous interest by the public concerning the recent promotion of homosexuality. Years ago, the TV show *Ellen* did the "unthinkable"—it openly addressed the lesbian lifestyle. There were mixed reactions as this type of show was transported into millions of homes across the country.

Currently, the media has attempted to outdo itself. Networks are competing with each other about who can come up with the most risqué show centered around homosexuality. "Gay" sells, and America is eating it up.

The report showed gay celebrities everywhere. It highlighted parades, festivals, and couples stating their commitments to join in mutual life-long partnership. It seems as though all is well for the homosexual "agenda."

Toward the end of the special report, the network interviewed a radical gay activist who wasn't too thrilled about the apparent success. He talked about his fear in this season of homosexual tolerance and propaganda. He shared his concern that the movement was creating a false sense of victory. Americans might think that gay TV programs are entertaining, but in reality, the majority of Americans think homosexuals are odd and irrelevant in relationship to societal norms. No American really takes the gay lifestyle seriously. He wondered if the homosexuals who were celebrating the victories were simply deceived and foolish.

I thought to myself, how true this is concerning the Christian subculture? We have Christian programming everywhere. There is Christian propaganda on every corner. Yet, I wonder, what's the effect? Do we have a false sense of victory? Is the world a better place? Are we winning the battle because Christian candy exists? Does the world just view believers as entertaining? Are we simply odd and irrelevant to them? Are we taken seriously? Are most of us simply deceived and foolish because we are celebrating false victories?

There are "good" things being done in the "name" of Christ. But, let's think critically for a second. What does a Christian phone book produce? It's a collection of people who verbally align themselves with a fairly conservative Christian creed. So what's the outcome?

Many times the Christian phone book directs other Christians to do business with other Christians. Is this our mission? After all, it is biblical to do good to those who are of the household of faith.[13] However, are we truly fulfilling God's will?

JESUS IN THE 'HOOD

I wonder what Christ would think of the Christian market if He were living in the flesh here on earth today. He would probably contemplate the current situation while driving in His car purchased from the Christian car dealership. Most definitely the back of His car would bear a new Christian bumper sticker.

He would be sipping on his Jesus Java that He picked up from the Christian coffeehouse. Of course He would be decked out with the latest Christian T-shirt—a "creative" knock-off of a "worldly" slogan. He would journal His thoughts in His Christian notebook with his Christian pencil that reads, "I'm a member of the J Team."

If He couldn't get a healthy perspective, maybe He could listen to some Christian music. If that didn't clear His head, He could always waltz into the local Christian bookstore. In fact, He might enjoy playing with a Jesus action figure. If His mind was still cloudy, He could gain some insight while walking the treadmill at the Christian fitness club.

Eventually, He'd become fatigued and need some Christian vitamins to help Him reenergize. All this walking in the world would probably wear Him out. He might enjoy kicking back on the sofa chewing some Christian candy while feasting on a healthy diet of Christian TV. If He got really hungry, He could always grab the Christian phone book and order out for a Christian pizza.

> **WE BECOME IRRELEVANT WHEN WE SEPARATE FROM THE WORLD AND REFUSE TO INTERFACE WITH THE PEOPLE IN IT.**

REACHING OUR GOAL

Is this our mission? Is our goal reached when we participate in every aspect of the market by providing a Christian alternative? It seems to me that all these alternatives collectively produce one common outcome. It seems they create a subculture that separates us further from the very people we are trying to reach. I don't recall God giving us the option to create an alternative subculture that retreats and hides out from the world.

One of the only reasons—if not THE only reason—God did not transport us to heaven the moment we got saved is because He gave us a job description that calls for us to be salt and light in a decaying and dark world.[14]

Salt seasons and salt preserves. Salt is only a preservative when it comes in contact with a rotting element. Salt only seasons when it comes in contact with something that needs seasoning. Salt has no effect when it's on a shelf. If salt is on the shelf, it's because it's irrelevant.

Likewise, we become irrelevant when we separate from the world and refuse to interface with the people in it. We no longer season or preserve our environment. Instead, we're merely absent from it. We sit on the shelf and shout our commentaries. As a result, the world continues to decay and remain in a place of tastelessness.

Have you ever seen a lamp turned on in a gymnasium filled with fluorescent lights? The lamp looks odd and serves no purpose when in an environment that's already well lit. The lamp only serves its purpose when it's within an environment that's dark. Light isn't meant to remain hidden. To be effective, it must branch out and rub shoulders with the darkness.

Similarly, followers of Jesus need to move out of the light and into the darkness. Was this not the model Christ set forth? He retreated from the religious institutions of His day. Instead, He went to the places of darkness in order to bring marvelous light.

Many youth pastors endorse separatism in very subtle ways. I know I have. We perpetuate a model to our youth that separatism is honorable. Each year at graduation, we often give extra special treatment to graduates who are going into full-time ministry or Christian colleges. Many churches give extra prayer, extra dollars, and extra time to spotlight those few brave students venturing into sacred fields or institutions.

No matter what we say, with these actions we confuse the Church of Christ. With our lip service, we teach that all believers are in full-time ministry. However, with our actions, we commission the few. Future generations sit in the pews and watch, feeling guilty if they dream of one day having a "secular" career.

We need to realize that spirituality goes well beyond career paths. In fact, God has viable ministries planned for people in secular fields. We need pastors. We need missionaries. But we also need thinkers, mechanics, painters, engineers, homemakers, and factory workers. Everywhere people are, the Church desperately needs a vibrant representation of Christ there as well. Therefore, every high school and college graduate needs to be commissioned as a full-time minister!

As I mentioned before, our spirituality must be incarnated into everyday life. When this takes place, geography or activity no longer bind spirituality. In other words, like Christ, we can interact with the world and still be spiritual. Our spirituality is not derived from where we go or what we do. We don't have to be separated from the world and in the church choir in order to maintain our holiness. This must be understood. If not, then Christianity is simply reduced to a building (church) and/or a day of the week (Sunday). This is what many believers are currently struggling with. They are localized Christians who are one-day worshipers.

> WITH OUR LIP SERVICE, WE TEACH THAT ALL BELIEVERS ARE IN FULL-TIME MINISTRY. HOWEVER, WITH OUR ACTIONS, WE COMMISSION THE FEW.

Francis Schaffer wrote, "A platonic concept of spirituality which does not include all of life is not true biblical spirituality. True spirituality touches all of life ... not just 'religious' things."[15]

Abraham Kuyper added onto this concept by stating, "There is not an inch in the entire domain of our human life of which Christ, who is sovereign of all, does not proclaim, 'Mine!'"[16]

Perhaps Martin Luther understood the true biblical potential for new Christians to impact their world for Christ. One day, during the Reformation period, a shoemaker came to Luther wondering if he should quit his job and take on a more "spiritual profession" since he was now a believer. Luther said, "make a good shoe and sell it at a fair price ... in this God is glorified."[17]

Luther cut through a million layers of fuzzy thinking in that one comment. In other words, our spirituality is not limited to a specific job, location, or livelihood. Rather, spirituality is with us wherever we go, because it should be who we are. Wherever we go, God is there. He is omnipresent. If we're in deep relationship with Him, our spirituality will flow out of that relationship, regardless of our activity.

Michael S. Horton, author of *Where in the World is the Church*, adds some great insight into this line of thinking: "When asked what Luther would do if he knew Christ was coming back tomorrow Luther replied, 'I would plant a tree.' In other words, God is so pleased with our ordinary, faithful activity in this world that Luther no longer felt that he had to be found in prayer or in 'spiritual' exercises when Christ returned in order to receive his blessing."[18]

Spirituality can be when you sit down to watch a movie or read a book. God doesn't disappear when we digest literature, art, and music that is secular. In fact, our spirituality doesn't disappear either. Obviously, we need to exercise caution. We need to beware of things that might master us or things that might not be lovely, beautiful, or noble.[19] However, just because something isn't "Christian" doesn't mean we should avoid it. In fact, God may intend for non-Christian things to play a role in our sanctification. It is through wrestling with issues wherein we become stronger and sharper. God wants us to wrestle with Him. That's what life is about—exercising faith and being in dynamic relationship, not static religion.

Too often categories become the lazy man's attempt at personal holiness. Categories often prevent holiness from showing up, because with categories, faith isn't necessary.

PREACHING TO THE CHOIR

Some of the efforts perpetuated by the separatist are commendable. After all, the world does produce some pretty rotten stuff at times. For example, some secular music glorifies rape, abuse, premarital sex, extramarital sex, and homosexuality. Obviously, feasting on this type of music is toxic to one's spiritual health.

But guess what?—there's bad Christian music out there too. This bad Christian music might even be slow and without drums (shocker). Bad Christian music mostly comes in the form of bad theology. By "bad theology," I'm referring to songs out on the market that present God in an unbiblical way. Perhaps they present a God who is merely accommodating or a God who wants to be your buddy and not your Lord. I'm much stricter on what comes into my ears with the name of Jesus stamped on it than with secular music I hear while in the mall. Why? Is that a double standard?

Anything that comes in the name of God is intended to affect and influence the way I think about Him. There are a lot of unbiblical and unorthodox views, teachings, and descriptions of God that come under the Christian label. This to me is a greater danger than blatant "secular" music, because it's often subtle and goes undetected.

Preachers who tell their congregation to follow the Berean model of searching the Scriptures, rather than obeying church lists of approved media, ought to be commended.[20] We need to enter the Christian bookstore with the same caution. In my opinion, the labels of "Christian" and "secular" have done just as much damage to the Church as good. There's a tendency among some believers to allow the labels of "Christian" and "secular" to become the discerning factors about what a person should or should not consume. Such practices dull our discernment and dependence on God.

THE LAW OF LOVE

The nation of Israel longed for a visible king to rule them, just like the other nations around. They didn't want an invisible God as their source of authority and guidance. Since very early on in history, man has desired clear-cut laws. Beginning with the Law on Mt. Sinai until present day, humanity has desired a rulebook to follow, rather than a relationship in which to be involved.

The Law was supposed to reveal sin and cause people to turn to God.[21] Ironically, when the Israelites were told about the Law, instead of admitting their inability to obey it and turning to God for help, they responded in an arrogant manner.

Then Moses came and recounted to the people all the words of the LORD and all the ordinances; and all the people answered with one voice, and said, "All the words which the LORD has spoken we will do!"[22]
—Exodus 24:3

Just in case God did not hear the Israelites correctly, they repeated if for Him. Who knows? Maybe they thought He was hard of hearing.

Then he took the book of the covenant and read it in the hearing of the people; and they said, "All that the LORD has spoken we will do, and we will be obedient!"
—*Exodus 24:7*

Notice it wasn't too long before the Israelites realized how much they could really do on their own. The human will to be holy doesn't last long on its own strength.

They have quickly turned aside from the way which I commanded them. They have made for themselves a molten calf, and have worshiped it, and have sacrificed to it, and said, "This is your god, O Israel, who brought you up from the land of Egypt!"
—*Exodus 32:8*

The Law was never instituted to replace relationship with God. Instead, it was created to increase relationship with God. Throughout history, people have missed the heart of the law and embraced the letter of the law. They use rules, lists, and religion as a means to keep themselves unstained by the world. When this becomes the focus, rather than God, sin is sure to follow.

On numerous occasions, God proclaimed His abhorrence for such a lifestyle. "What are your multiplied sacrifices to me? I have had enough of burnt offerings of rams and the fat of fed cattle. And I take no pleasure in the blood of bulls, lambs, or goats."[23]

Many times the Israelites had all the right actions. Their deeds were blameless, just like the Pharisees. However, they were missing the whole love relationship with God. God's greatest desire is that His people love Him holistically.[24] Jesus hit the heart of this separatism when He said, "I desire mercy and not sacrifice."[25]

ABOVE THE LAW

There is a fine line between "being in the world and not of it." Discovering much of what this means is something God intends for He and you to wrestle through. That is the beauty of biblical faith. In areas of Christian liberty, there is no blanket standard that applies to all people.[26]

Many churches and Christian movements have attempted to spell out what books, movies, music, art forms, and poetry are acceptable. This is simply resurrected legalism. This is often what you and I want. We want a checklist of do's and don'ts that we can post up on our wall. We want a list of rules to nail others with when they fail to measure up. There's a nasty voice inside us that longs to cry out and tell another brother or sister in Christ, "You failed!"

We all want to know there is someone out there who is a little dirtier, a little uglier, and a little more "in need of grace." We like to convince ourselves that we're not quite as bad as the guy next door.

God wants more. He wants us to personally wrestle with Him, because He knows us best. He wants us to form our own convictions and not just adopt our neighbor's. He wants us to stand approved. To make someone else's convictions our own is to avoid relationship with God. He desires this relationship with you and me so much that He sacrificed His own Son. He is just as concerned about the process of forming your convictions as He is about the convictions you end up holding.

There is no fear in love; but perfect love casts out fear, because fear involves
punishment, and the one who fears is not perfected in love.
—1 John 4:18

Numbing the Void
January 2000

Sing me songs. Fabricate fables. Repeat rhymes.
I'm too codependent to care.
Both diseased with these plagues that create
diagnostic anthologies of pride and passion, interspersed
with emotions half-felt, and dreams half-lived.
Yeah, I bought the beauty, that mirage of nirvana
that whispered its promises that it couldn't deliver.
Numbing the void I settle for pieces of fragment
in the form of splinters and strands. Exhausted,
I liquefy into otherworldly plains of transcendence.

Ignorant masses pound out their songs of forgotten
foolishness. Popular culture claims its tolerance,
its fragrance of individuality leaves me cursed with
putrid confessions of incompetence. None friends.
No solace. Free from peace and rest and all other
shreds of unbelievable happenstance. I am released as
I let go and fall into apathy.

CHAPTER 5=
THE CONFORMISTS

"WASTE NO MORE TIME ARGUING WHAT A GOOD MAN
SHOULD BE. BE ONE."

—*Marcus Aurelius*

IF YOU'RE like me, you grew up knowing you should never rip on someone else's girl. This is a fact of life. You could talk about someone's lack of football skills, wrestling talent, or even academic efforts, but you should never speak negatively of somebody's girlfriend. To do so meant an immediate audience in the guy's bathroom in between classes for a scuffle that made *Braveheart* look like documentary on world peace.

You'd think I would have learned that. However, a couple years ago, I found myself beginning to badmouth somebody else's girl. The first time it happened, I was sitting in a coffee shop with a few of my buddies. I didn't intentionally bring it up; it just sort of happened. We somehow got on the topic of a guy we all knew. Pretty soon we started to talk about his girl, and negative comments started flying.

I felt kind of bad for the guy. We all liked him; he was our friend. His girl just really annoyed the heck out of us. Maybe we were insecure or hurt. Maybe that's why we started throwing around the comments. Who knows?

I walked away from the coffee shop that night feeling pretty low. The conversation had been entertaining, but at the same time, I felt really convicted. There was something twisted about such a strange amount of pleasure coming from ripping on this girl.

I suppose degrading this girl was pleasurable because it made us feel separate from her. After all, nobody wanted to be associated with a loser. So, next week, same time, my buddies and I started to talk about our friend's girl again. Only this time it became more intense. What first started as dislike now evolved into hatred.

We started to talk around the table about how this girl offended us. She didn't dress right or know how to talk right. The music she liked was too old school. It was kind of addicting hearing each other's intellectual commentaries about the deficiencies of this girl.

I think the problem was that this girl was so ugly. It was an ugliness that was both internal and external. She was really out of date. I suppose you could use the word irrelevant. She just didn't fit in. Nobody wanted her around. In fact, we all felt ashamed to say we even knew her, much less that we used to hang out with her.

It went on like this for several months. In fact, more people knew this girl than I first thought. It became an opening line to talk about this girl. I even went to parties and initially met people by communicating my distaste and shame for this girl.

Then one day I ran into her guy. It was not cool, let me tell you. I didn't expect to see Him. I just kind of bumped into Him. He turned around and just looked me in the eye. He said to me, "Kary, why? How could you talk about her like that?"

I felt really low. I could see how much He loved her, and I could feel how much I hated her. I guess I just felt wounded by her. I felt judged by her. I said, "Jesus, I am sorry I spoke about your Bride like that. I'm not really sure why I have so much bitterness for your Church."

Are You?

THE TRAGIC TREND

I've seen a trend lately. A lot of people are walking around with a lot of bitterness toward the Church. In fact, pockets of people have organized times to complain about how the Church has disrespected them. Some of her offenses may have come in the form of legalism, religiosity, or condemnation.

Throughout history, the Church has been dressed in many different clothes. Sometimes she is relevant and beautiful, adorned in the finest and most elegant apparel. At other times she is in rags. She is strung out in the gutter of irrelevance. It kind of reminds me how I must look to Jesus many times.

Nonetheless, to my wonderment, Jesus never loses His passion for His Bride (or for you and I for that matter). His Church is still on His heart. Thus, His Church needs to be on our hearts. There is no other Bride. We are it. We can't escape each other, so we might as well reconcile with each other. If we're badmouthing God's girl, then we're diametrically opposed to what's on His heart.

I see a potential threat on the horizon. If wounded people fail to move through their pain into a process of healing and convert their energies into something positive, an entire generation could be wasted on just sitting around and complaining about the Church's irrelevance.

Many wounded believers have been involved in a knee-jerk reaction against the Church. They been burned by the Church and her separatist tendencies, and so they overcompensate by claiming full allegiance to culture and loving people.

These believers vow never to be sucked into a man-made organized religion again. They want to be free. They want to escape law, rules, and dead faith. Although their intentions may be pure, irrelevant tendencies often creep into their hearts if they're not too careful. Because many of these people alienate themselves from a community of faith (whether or not they admit it), they end up conforming to culture rather than transforming culture. While their motives to be relevant with the rest of the world are honorable, they tend to become unbalanced very quickly.

Many have reacted against their church experience, which taught them to separate from the world and culture. Others never got sucked into separatist tendencies because their intuitive nature allowed them to see the obvious hypocrisy perpetuated by some church leadership. As a result, they now waltz through culture feasting on the world, not ever thinking to filter the truth from the toxic. As a reaction against separatism, they simply take it all in.

DECEIVED PEOPLE LOVERS

Referring back to our paradigm, let's take a look at how conformists' faith and culture are unbalanced from their love for God and people.

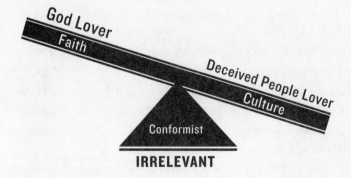

Figure 5.I - The Irrelevant Conformist

Conformists, in their pursuit of relevance, justify themselves as people lovers, deceive themselves, and often become an offense to God. You can spot a conformist a mile a way. They claim to love God, but their "strong" stance for consuming culture alienates them from people and God. They are completely irrelevant.

So where do conformists get fuel for their fire? Interestingly enough, they pick random verses out of context while failing to examine the whole of Scripture. They approach the Bible with a preconceived grid that allows them to see what they want to see.[1] They cling to these verses as proof that God wants them to be immersed in all aspects of culture. In fact, many believe with all their hearts that they are doing this in order to be people lovers. Below is some of the often-used ammo in the arsenal of the conformist:

*For everything created by God is good,
and nothing is to be rejected, if it is received with gratitude ... —1 Timothy 4:4*

Why is my freedom judged by another's conscience? —1 Corinthians 10:29

The earth is the LORD's, and all it contains ... —Psalm 24:1

For the world is Mine, and all it contains. —Psalm 50:12

*The heavens are Thine, the earth also is Thine;
The world and all it contains, Thou hast founded them. —Psalm 89:11*

*And He said to them, "Are you so lacking in understanding also? Do you not understand that whatever goes into the man from outside cannot defile him; because it does not go into his heart, but into his stomach, and is eliminated?" (Thus He declared all foods clean.) And He was saying, "That which proceeds out of the man, that is what defiles the man."
—Mark 7:18-20*

*To those who are without law, as without law, though not being without the law of God but under the law of Christ, that I might win those who are without law.
To the weak I became weak, that I might win the weak;*

I have become all things to all men, that I may by all means save some.
—1 Corinthians 9:21-22

MIRROR, MIRROR ON THE WALL

Like separatism, conformity cuts so deep. How do we unwrap the many layers that characterize this irrelevant extreme? For starters, let's examine ourselves in the mirror that reflects our spiritual condition and see how we look.

Many components contribute to someone being characterized as one who struggles with conformity. However, when we look at a conformist, often time three common traits rise to the surface. A conformist allows 1) media to replace meditation, 2) liberty to replace love, and 3) tolerance to replace truth.

How do you look? Do you struggle with any of these? If you're honest, do you spend more time catching up with popular culture, rather than being still before the Lord? Do you find yourself justifying behavior because you have a "right to"? Do you fail to love others enough to consider how they might interpret your actions? Do you find yourself tolerating untruth because you don't want to appear narrow-minded or judgmental?

If any of these are remotely true about you, then you probably struggle with tendencies of conformity. Like I've said before, in my own life at different times concerning different issues, I've found I struggle with both the tendencies of a separatist or a conformist, sometimes even in the same day. Maybe you will find the same to be true.

Remember, if you're a separatist and you're thinking this chapter doesn't apply to you, read it anyway. Understanding this chapter will allow you to get into a conformist's thought patterns. This is the first step toward the healing process that must take place within our current Church age.

If you're a conformist, take this chapter at a slow pace. The examples given are intentionally extreme. This has been done in order to demonstrate the incorrect thinking patterns and courses of actions that characterize the conformist. Remember, this part of the journey may be difficult. Few of us enjoy looking into the mirror when, at the present moment, we appear pretty irrelevant.

CHAMELEONS OF CULTURE

Conformists are the more "enlightened" ones. They hate separatists and the rules they impose. They see separatists as the backward folk who embrace monastic traditions by retreating from the evil world.

Conformists parade their "liberty" for all to see. They push the line and the limit, not because they necessarily believe in the activities, but for shock value. They justify the most extreme forms of media, movies and music in order "to become all things to all people." In fact, it's because they love people that they willingly subject themselves to every form of pleasure.

They feast on an hourly diet of MTV, justifying the need to know the world they are trying to reach. Their lives are marked by addictions to substances that were originally only a "tool" for evangelism.

The Bible seems a little too intolerant. Conformists prefer supplemental reading from other walks of spiritualism, in order to relate with their world. They bash the Bride of Christ (the Church) in coffee shop talks with other conformists. In fact, the conformist that can throw the best punch at separatists often gets the best applause from his or her fellow conformists.

Loving God has been reduced to surfing the Net for spiritual topics. Boundaries in the areas of thought life and dating have eroded to nothing in an attempt to boast tolerance for other philosophical bents.

Conformists try to think like the world, dress like the world, and act like the world in order to reach the world. After all, the worst thing to be is irrelevant. Conformists have such a love for people that they'd enjoy burning separatists at the stake for the legalistic standards they shove down people's throats.

TAKING IT ALL IN

As a reaction against the separatist who denies many worldly things, the conformist simply takes it all in. The motto of the separatist is to reject all things. The motto of the conformist is to accept all things.

They're so fearful of being archaic that they blindly consume all things.

Soon their diet catches up with them, and they begin looking more and more like the audience they're trying to reach. This may sound good at first. After all, many effective missionaries adopted the customs and culture of the people they were trying to reach. Unfortunately, many conformists simply become unbalanced. They lose their focus and mission. They're merely reactionaries.

Instead of conformists being salt, the world realizes they taste just like them. Instead of conformists being light, the world realizes they look just like them. In their attempt to be relevant, they become irrelevant. Because culture is always changing, conformists are always changing. As a result, conformists are unknowingly in an eternal identity crisis. They're never quite sure who they are or what they believe, so they simply reflect culture instead of transform it.

FORSAKING THE ASSEMBLY

Let us not give up meeting together, as some are in the habit of doing, but let us encourage one another—and all the more as you see the Day approaching.
—Hebrews 10:25 (NIV)

Conformists often "get killed" out in the world because they have no community of faith. Many conformists are independent wounded sheep who have been bitten by other sheep. The last thing they want to do is hang around with more sheep. Organized church scares them, and so they wander out on their own to face the big world.

I understand this tendency. I just don't agree with it. If the only church available is a church filled with legalistic separatists, then by all means separate from the separatists! Nonetheless, every believer needs to be involved in a community of faith. These communities probably look a lot different than the traditional church many of us grew up attending. They don't need to meet in a building or have an order of service.

The trend among many young adults is to just be floaters. They're not sure why they attend a church, but they think it's something they should do. So, for a time, they causally try out churches. They may even commit to attending a church. But, every church has its warts, and soon they become disillusioned and quit assembling.

At one point in my life, I became disillusioned with the Church. I saw its gossip, legalism, and petty rule-based religiosity. I attended out of duty for several months. Then I decided to become part of the solution rather than part of the problem. I decided to stop looking at my needs and how the Church was not meeting them. I saw a vast number of wounded believers who were just as tired and fed up as me. I decided I would try to serve them.

> **ANYONE CAN COMPLAIN AND WALLOW IN THEIR WOUNDS. GET UP AND BE PART OF THE SOLUTION.**

I quickly found out there were needs all around. Sure, the Church has warts. After all, it's filled with people like you and me. Regardless, there is no perfect church. I think God must have a sense of humor. He knew I had given up on the Church so much, and ironically, He decided to have me work in one.

WHICH ONE?

I'm not sure which church God wants you to be a part of. In fact, you may need to start your own. Why not? If the churches around you are so archaic and filled with separatism, then assemble your own gathering of believers. You might see how difficult it is to have a community of faith who are transformists.

Just do something productive. It's so easy to be a conformist who is critical and cynical of the Church. Anyone can complain and wallow in their wounds. Get up and be part of the solution. Create a global movement of transformists within your sphere of influence.[2]

Why am I sold on the Church?[3] First and foremost, because Jesus is passionate about her. If I am not passionate about His Bride, then I'm diametrically opposed to what's on His heart. Last time I checked, it's not a good thing to be diametrically opposed to something the God of the universe is passionate about.

Ironically, you've been uniquely created to have some of your needs met though a community of faith. Just like a marriage relationship, your needs will not be met by demanding them. Rather, they're met in the process of relationship. Many people start by asking the wrong question. They approach the conversation by demanding, "How can you meet my needs?"

When we commit to a community of faith and meet the needs of that community, strangely our own needs are met. As the paradox goes, when we seek to serve, we are served.

There are hundreds of reasons to be involved in a community of faith. For starters, I'm quickly going to list three that have intrinsically affected my walk of faith. They are: 1) Exercise of spiritual gifts, which provides purpose; 2) Accountability with one another, which provides significance; and 3) Encouragement of the saints, which provides transcendence.

Let's unpack these, one at a time.

EXERCISE—spiritual gifts (which provides purpose)

Imagine a day without your eyes. Think of twenty-four hours without your legs or nose or ears. What would it be like? Your whole body would suffer because a few of your body parts were missing. You would be severely limited in the way you could function. Life would be difficult and frustrating. In a short amount of time, you would be longing for your missing body parts.

The Bible says the Church is the Body of Christ. It's made up of individual members who corporately make up the Body. Each part has a specific task that benefits the rest of the Body. Every believer has an important and necessary purpose. When those parts are missing, the whole Body is incomplete and suffers.

However, when fellowship occurs and people are practicing their spiritual gifts, the whole Body functions in an effective way. Each part is extremely important. Each believer needs the uniqueness every other believer brings to the Body.

So in Christ we who are many form one body,
and each member belongs to all the others.
—Romans 12:5 (NIV)

We each have a significant and distinct gift of grace that blesses the rest of the Body. When we fail to assemble, we actually rob the Body of Christ!

As each one has received a special gift, employ it in serving one another,
as good stewards of the manifold grace of God.
—*1 Peter 4:10*

ACCOUNTABILITY—with one another (which provides significance)

A community of faith provides accountability. It's within relationships that we can share struggles and express genuine concern for others. Accountability allows men and women to let down their guard and ask for help. It's a framework that allows for authenticity. When we cut ourselves off from other believers, we set ourselves up to fail.

Iron sharpens iron, So one man sharpens another.
—*Proverbs 27:17*

Accountability invites relationship. It gives permission for others, who have our best interest in mind, to ask questions about how we are honestly doing in our marriages, friendships, thought life, devotional life, prayer life, and life itself! It allows concern without condemnation. There is nothing "biblical" about believers having to face the battle alone. As we function within a relationship that allows for accountability, we begin to understand the significant role we play in the life of another.

ENCOURAGEMENT—of the saints (which provides transcendence)

Encouragement literally means, "to give courage." Courage comes from the Latin word "core," which means "heart." To have courage means to have heart. When we lose courage, we lose heart.

And when we heard it, our hearts melted and no courage remained in any man any longer
because of you; for the LORD your God,
He is God in heaven above and on earth beneath.
—*Joshua 2:11*

To some people, it might be a strange thought that gathering with a community of faith is a process that can actually give courage. As believers, we're in a battle (Ephesians 6). Many times in the battle, we're tempted to give up. Hearing other believer's stories of God's faithfulness in their trials can actually give us courage to persevere through our own trials.

Fear often threatens to kill our courage. When we allow fear to creep into our hearts, it will begin to paralyze us. Ambrose Redmoon said, "Courage is not the absence of fear, but rather the judgment that something else is more important than fear."[4] The ancients described fear or lack of courage as having weak or feeble knees.

> *Therefore, strengthen the hands that are weak and the knees that are feeble ...*
> *—Hebrews 12:12*

This description makes sense. Regarding the battlefield, someone who has courage stands his ground firmly. The fearful one buckles under the pressure. When we assemble with our community of faith, one of the main ways we can bless others is through encouragement. Although seemingly small, a word of encouragement can breathe fresh air into someone's weary soul.

> *Encourage the exhausted, and strengthen the feeble. Say to those with anxious heart,*
> *"Take courage, fear not. Behold, your God will come with vengeance;*
> *The recompense of God will come, But He will save you."*
> *—Isaiah 35:3-4*

Literally, this means that words are what encourage others to strengthen their knees and keep fighting the battle. When we fellowship with other believers, words are exchanged. These words can be in the form of prayers, stories, talk, compliments, or the Word of God. Gathering in a community of faith, where redeeming words are exchanged, is a powerful way we can encourage others.

Your words have helped the tottering to stand,
And you have strengthened feeble knees.
—Job 4:4

The Lord God has given Me the tongue of disciples, That I may know how to sustain the
weary one with a word. He awakens Me morning by morning,
He awakens My ear to listen as a disciple.
—Isaiah 50:4

WHAT ABOUT CONFORMIST CHURCHES?

The trend within some churches today is to blindly infuse secular ideals, philosophies, and worldviews into the DNA of the Church. When the Bride of Christ turns from her groom Jesus Christ as the sole source of guidance and instead worships the ways of the world, she subtly commits spiritual adultery. When we adopt man's philosophies with the message of the Gospel, we allow syncretism to take place.

Paul was concerned with a vibrant jealously that the Church be presented spotless and blameless to her bridegroom Christ. Paul was committed to the purity of the Gospel and to the doctrines associated with it. In fact, he was so passionate about truth that he made the preservation and proclamation of it his life mission.

For I am jealous for you with a godly jealousy; for I betrothed you to one husband,
that to Christ I might present you as a pure virgin. But I am afraid, lest as the serpent
deceived Eve by his craftiness, your minds should be led astray from the simplicity and
purity of devotion to Christ.
For if one comes and preaches another Jesus whom we have not preached,
or you receive a different spirit which you have not received,
or a different gospel which you have not accepted, you bear this beautifully.
—2 Corinthians 11:2-4

Think back for a second to the Titanic. What made it sink? You might think the Titanic sunk because it hit an iceberg. This is not true. The reason it sunk was because too much water from the ocean came into the boat.

Think about the Church for a second. What threatens to sink it? You might think the Church is threatened to sink because of persecution. This is not true. The reason it's threatened to sink is because we are letting too much of the world's philosophy into the Church. Many churches, in an attempt to be relevant with the watching world, incarnate an improper definition of relevance.

As a result, the message of the Gospel is changed and compromised. Instead of the intended outcome—a relevant message—irrelevance emerges in its place.

> *See to it that no one takes you captive through philosophy and empty deception,*
> *according to the tradition of men, according to the elementary principles of*
> *the world, rather than according to Christ.*
> *—Colossians 2:8*

The world system does have a philosophy. It has a goal to set itself against the purposes of God. The Church has, in recent days, allowed such a system to creep in through the back door.

> *For our struggle is not against flesh and blood, but against the rulers, against*
> *the powers, against the world forces of this darkness, against the spiritual forces of*
> *wickedness in the heavenly places.*
> *—Ephesians 6:12*

> *We are destroying speculations and every lofty thing raised up against the knowledge of*
> *God, and we are taking every thought captive to the obedience of Christ ...*
> *—2 Corinthians 10:5*

There are not only biblical doctrines that exist, but also doctrines of demons. We're not in a neutral situation. We're in a battlefield and a war zone. We need to set our attention on modeling ourselves after biblical principles and practices.

But the Spirit explicitly says that in later times some will fall away from the faith,
paying attention to deceitful spirits and doctrines of demons ...
—1 Timothy 4:1

Satan doesn't come in a red suit and pitchfork. No, he comes to the Church in a very clever way, in an attempt to seduce her away from the truth. Often, our temptation is to model ourselves strictly after the

MANY CHURCHES, IN AN ATTEMPT TO BE RELEVANT WITH THE WATCHING WORLD, INCARNATE AN IMPROPER DEFINITION OF RELEVANCE.

secular framework, merely because it proves to be current or trendy.

For the time will come when they will not endure sound doctrine; but wanting to have their
ears tickled, they will accumulate for themselves teachers in accordance to their own desires;
and will turn away their ears from the truth, and will turn aside to myths.
—2 Timothy 4:3-4

NONCONFORMIST? NOT A CHANCE!

Several months ago, I was dialoguing with an individual about the whole transformed mind paradigm. For the sake of illustration, I will call him Tom. I didn't know Tom well, but as we spoke, many red flags surfaced. It was obvious that Tom was severely fed up and put off with being part of a community of faith. I asked Tom if he felt like he struggled with the tendencies that categorized a conformist or a separatist.

I was surprised by his response. In my mind, according to his life story, it seemed like he had conformist tendencies. Tom proudly said, "I consider myself to be a nonconformist. In fact, I'm extremely independent. I pride myself in being different than popular culture."

I asked him to tell me more. Through his statements, it was apparent to me that he was a full-blown conformist. I'll admit, his initial response of being a nonconformist took me by surprise. I wondered for a moment if in drafting the transformed mind paradigm, I had not accounted for this breed of people. However, God very quickly revealed to me that nonconformity is the very trend of current culture.

We live in a culture that boasts above all else about its tolerance. Everyone does what is right in his own eyes. This worldview, in and of itself, instructs people to conform to being a nonconformist. As a result, we're mass-producing nonconformists. The thing to be is a nonconformist. In fact, by being self-proclaimed nonconformists, ironically we label ourselves as conformists! For by claiming the status of nonconformity, we simply conform to current culture.

Although wrapped in the cloak of unique individuality, nonconformists are simply self-deceived that they're different than the rest. Although subtle, this is conformity in its truest sense.

Throughout history, different eras were defined by what was popular or in style. I imagine in the Middle Ages, there was a popular line of armor to wear or a certain style of sword to fight with. Especially in the last one hundred years, each generation labeled what was and wasn't cool. If one wanted to be relevant, then he or she conformed to the understood standard of "relevance."

These days, everything seems to be cool or "relevant." If you want to be attracted to guys, that's cool. If you want to be attracted to girls, that's cool. If you want to be attracted to both, that's cool. Claim to worship the stars. That's cool. Claim to worship yourself. That's cool. Claim to worship pleasure. That's cool. Everything is cool, except for intolerance or absolute truth.

Do whatever you want. Be different from everybody else. Just don't tell me what to be or what to do, and everything is cool. Conform to being a nonconformist.

Conformists often fail to stand strongly for anything. As a result, they fall for most everything. They build their worldview around accepting all philosophy, all media, and all doctrine. Thus, when it all comes down, they fall because their roots are shallow and their purpose is fickle.

From the outside, nonconformists seem extremely accommodating and accepting. However, when push comes to shove, deviating from tolerance will soon cause the nonconformist to become extremely intolerant.

Tom hung himself with his very words. He identified himself as being a radical conformist simply by stating his "nonconformist" status. There is only one option to withdrawing from culture or immersing oneself in culture. There is only one alternative to being a conformist or a separatist. Only a small remnant has the courage to transform culture. But this remnant is growing.

> *Act as free men, and do not use your freedom as a covering for evil,*
> *but use it as bondslaves of God.*
> *—1 Peter 2:16*

Your Language.
December 1999

You fall. I follow.
You lead. I love.
You live. I lose.

All of who I am seeks to adhere to a dream
A moment, a belief so big, so true
It's what I am, what I've always
Known, but never dared to pursue

I dream. You die.
I fail. You free.
I breathe. You build.

Release, empower, encourage, you reach within and
Draw without things that society criticized. Aspects
That legalists condemn. Pieces that Pharisees ridicule
And fears had silenced. And fatigue destroyed those facets
That you labeled beautiful and unique.

You burn. I begin.
You float. I fly.
You transcend. I travel.

Your bravery blows my mind. You've shown me so
Much. Standing on the edge of all I knew, I convinced
Myself that this was all there is. In a way where logic
Stopped, emotions began. And I needed someone who
Believed. Who dared to go with me where I

Had not gone myself, where I knew not
Existed.

I run. You rejoice.
I see. You soar.
I perceive. You presumed.

CHAPTER 6=
THE TRANSFORMISTS

"IN ANOTHER MOMENT DOWN WENT ALICE AFTER IT,
NEVER ONCE CONSIDERING HOW IN THE WORLD SHE
WAS TO GET OUT AGAIN."

—*Lewis Carroll*[1]

WE LIVE in a day and age where directions are easier to find than ever before. Thanks to MapQuest, even those of us who are directionally challenged no longer have an excuse. Even the most casual Internet user can feel power at his fingertips when seeking for directions to get across the country or just across town. If you know the starting point and intended destination, the directions for how to get there are only a few clicks away.

Unfortunately, when one sets out for the destination of relevance, directions are not that simple. To our dismay, MapQuest doesn't offer a road that leads to relevance. I tried to pursue that option during some troubled times in my journey.

In theory, the road to relevance is very simple. It's merely paved with loving God and loving people. Thus, in one way, it looks the same for every sojourner. On the other hand, the specific steps, the curves in your road, and the detours God has planned are unique to you individually. Therefore, your exact road appears different from anybody else's road.

If in theory, it's so easy to be relevant, then why is there so much fog that prevents us from reaching our destination of a transformed mind? Maybe, it's because so few people have ever made it there alive. Maybe it's because those who made it never want to leave to go tell others how to get there. Maybe the road is so dangerous that few ever venture to find it.

Hopefully, the last few chapters have exposed some irrelevant tendencies that seek to prevent you from continuing your journey. Before we could move ahead, we first had to examine where we've been. Now that we've become familiar with the irrelevant extremes of the separatist and conformist, let's examine the life of the transformist.

STANDING FOR SOMETHING

I believe the message of being relevant is long overdue. It's been refreshing to bask in the truth it bears. However, if our generation is going to draw a line in the sand against dead orthodoxy and heartless religion, then we better know not only what we are turning from, but also what we are turning to in its place. If we only define what we're turning from and fail to define what we are turning to, then we just become a bunch of mindless fools with a lot of passion. Believe me, I've been in that camp more times than I wish to admit.

If we hope to start a movement, if we hope to transform culture, we need to be a gathering that stands for something. It's so easy to just be against everything. Many of us are against legalism or traditional church or dead orthodoxy. The question that deserves just as much attention—if not more—is, "What do we stand for?"

The rest of this book is an examination of the life of the transformist. Who is he? What does she stand for? What is the road that leads to this type of relevant person who transcends the here and now? How does he face culture? How does she stay balanced? What allows a transformist to integrate his faith with the world around him? Most importantly, how can the life of a transformist be incarnated into everyday life?

JOINING THE RANKS

I believe we need to resurrect an ancient/cutting-edge gathering of believers who transcend the irrelevant life of the separatist and conformist. Since the time of Abel, there has been a movement of people who neither conformed to culture nor separated from culture. Sometimes this movement has been strong. Sometimes it's struggled. Sometimes there have been few and other times many. Regardless, their testimony has stood the test of time, and from the grave, they still speak.[2]

I believe this gathering needs to know who they are and where they're going. They don't need to have everything figured out, for that would mean they are separatists. They don't need to say anything goes, for that would mean they are conformists.

This gathering is not perfect, for none of us are. However, they're seekers. They long to have a simple and unadulterated relationship with the Creator of the universe. They desire to know the "why" behind the "what" and the purpose behind the principle. Of course there will be mistakes along the way, but this is what sets these believers apart. This gathering has a little more grace and patience with each other, because they know what they have been saved from.

The movement is beginning. The gathering of believers has united. They come from a variety of backgrounds but share a common purpose. Above all else, they passionately love God and people in proper balance. They're not afraid of culture because their mission transcends it. They're not afraid of religion because their method surpasses it. They are the relevant. They are the transformists.

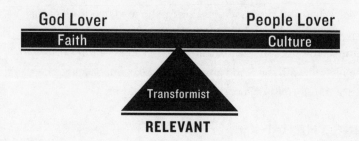

Figure 6.1 - The Relevant Transformist

POSTER CHILD FOR SEPARATISM

So what does a transformist look like? What are the practical strategies he or she might use to work within culture and not against it? What are some biblical guidelines that shed light upon this faithful remnant? Was there anyone in Scripture who exhibited a healthy balance in this arena, or are transformists merely the stuff of fairytales and folklore?

Let's examine the life of one transformist. Let's probe into his thought process and wielding of culture. Let's look at his love for God and love for people. Let's look at the Apostle Paul.

Outside of Jesus Christ, Paul was one of the most relevant people in all of Scripture. Originally, Paul could have been the poster child for the separatist camp. Maybe this is why, in the end, he became such a powerful transformist. He not only knew where he'd come from, but also what he'd been saved from as well. His irrelevant extremes were exposed in a very public way.[3]

After Paul journeyed through his irrelevant tendencies, he emerged as a man who was completely relevant. Relevance was not a status he attained. Rather, it was a quality of life he maintained only through his relationship with God.

Relevance became the main facet of Paul's evangelistic strategy. Paul says he became all things to all men, so that he might save some.[4] This sounds like someone who is unbalanced. Doesn't this fit the language of a conformist?

Notice the verses that follow. "I run in such a way, not without aim, I box in such a way, as not beating the air; but I discipline my body and make it my slave, so that after I have preached to others, I myself will not be disqualified."[5] This also sounds like someone who is unbalanced. Doesn't this fit the language of a separatist?

Paul, the transformist, balanced loving God with loving people. He walked on the edge of enjoying and redeeming culture. He even used culture for ministry purposes, yet was careful not to be disqualified by it.

> PAUL, THE TRANSFORMIST, BALANCED LOVING GOD WITH LOVING PEOPLE. HE WALKED ON THE EDGE OF ENJOYIING AND REDEEMING CULTURE.

But how? That line is so thin. The potential for destruction is so real. How does Paul maintain a pure conscience while participating in culture at the same time?

THE BALANCED BOY

Paul was not a novice when it came to biblical learning. He was no stranger to the Scriptures. After his preliminary education, at the age of thirteen, he most likely attended the premiere Jewish school of sacred learning in Jerusalem. It was there that he became a student of the renowned rabbi Gamaliel. Paul spent much of his time in dialogue with the religiously educated of the day. In fact, very possibly, he later became a member of the Great Sanhedrin. Following his conversion, he spent at least three years in the Arabian Desert sitting under the teaching of the Spirit of Christ.[6]

Interestingly enough, Paul was also not a novice in cultural learning. His hometown Tarsus, of which he was not only a resident, but also a citizen, "surpassed all other universities, such as Alexandria and Athens, in the study of philosophy and educational literature in general."[7] Tarsus was an integrated city, a melting pot of sorts, with music, culture, and literature from many parts of the known world. "As a citizen of Tarsus, Paul was a citizen of the whole world."[8]

Paul, a transformist, knew God and the Word that was able to save souls.[9] Paul, a transformist, knew people and the culture in which they lived. He was committed to both audiences and compromised neither.

PRACTICAL PAYS

Let's see how Paul practically incarnated the life of a transformist. Let's look at how his balanced life was fleshed out, especially in a time when culture was far from being Christian.[10]

When Paul was waiting for Silas and Timothy in the Greek City of Athens, he didn't hide out from culture. Instead, he moved throughout it. He took his faith to the marketplace. He didn't see culture as the enemy. Paul saw a city full of idols. In fact, a Roman satirist said it was "easier to find a god in Athens than a man."

A separatist would have hung out in the hotel at Athens, read the Scriptures, and waited for fellow missionaries Timothy and Silas (something I probably would've done). A conformist would have hit the streets and indulged in culture without any thought of redeeming it. Paul, the transformist, took a more balanced approach. He took in culture, but not to the extreme that he was compromised by it. Rather, he studied the culture in order to transform the culture with the life-changing message of Jesus Christ.

Paul daily reasoned with the Jews, the God-fearing Gentiles, and anyone else who happened to be present.[11] He preached the Lord Jesus Christ and the resurrection.

Soon the city was buzzing with talk of a strange preacher who preached strange gods. The Athenians took Paul to the philosophical hot spot of the day called Aeropagus. Even the name *aareos* (which means sensual pleasure) and *pagus* (which relates to sorcery or witchcraft) reflects the darkness that surrounded the location. Aeropagus was the supreme tribunal of ancient

Athens that began as the king's council by the Draco code of Law in 621 B.C.[11] Basically Aeropagus (the Latin form of the Greek word, translated Mars' Hill) was the location of pagan temples where philosophers gathered each day to discuss, argue, and learn new ideas.

Paul, the transformist who loved God and people, the man committed to the purity of the Gospel and the use of culture, spoke a relevant message that all his listeners could comprehend. He gained favor with his audience by acknowledging, not bashing or devaluing, their philosophical and religious bents.[12] Paul cited two Greek poems, one by Epimenides and one by Aratus of Soli. He used quotations from their literature and familiar phrases from their language.

> PAUL STUDIED THE CULTURE IN ORDER TO TRANSFORM THE CULTURE WITH THE LIFE-CHANGING MESSAGE OF JESUS CHRIST.

Paul learned their culture, their literature, their common places, their marketplaces, and their holy places. He understood the city's layout, the city's philosophy, and the city's religion. He used all that knowledge about the people, motivated by his love for the people, before uttering a word about His God.

However, once he spoke, he didn't pull any punches. He realized that identifying with their culture could only bring them to a certain point. It could help him gain common ground with the Greeks, but it couldn't make dead people turn to life or sinners turn to saints. The Athenians needed to hear the life-changing message of Jesus Christ and Him crucified.

Paul was very accommodating, but he drew a line in the sand. He said, "What therefore you worship in ignorance, this I proclaim to you."[13] He went on to introduce them to the God who made everything, gives life, ordains the position of men, judges men, and raised His Son from the dead.

Notice the outcome of being relevant. Some mocked. Some believed. Some asked him to come back and speak more. Paul walked the line between loving God and loving people. As a result, he drew a line that caused his listeners to respond. He didn't receive applause. In fact, he received some sneers. But, this transformist remained true to the message and the mission. He used culture and enjoyed culture without being compromised by it, while at the same time, shared the timeless truth of the Gospel.

IT MUST HAVE BEEN LOVE

As we learned earlier, relevance is really all about love. As we examine Acts 17, we see Paul's actions are centered around and motivated by his love for God and people. Love is the key to being relevant. If you're like me, love sounds so weak and powerless when mentioned in the context of the quest for relevance. Is our paradigm wrong, or are we wrong?

Maybe, in the context of relevance, the reason why love for God and love for people seems trite is because you and I have no clue what love truly is. Maybe we have no idea what it means to love God with all our heart, soul, and mind. Maybe we have no concept of what it means to love our neighbor as ourselves. Maybe, we need to take a rest stop on our road to relevance in order to process the transforming effects of love.

We know love by this that He laid down His life for us; and we ought to lay down our lives for the brethren. But whoever has the world's goods, and beholds his brother in need and closes his heart against him, how does the love of God abide in him?
—1 John 3:16-17

MY JOURNAL IN THE JOURNEY

Ripples My Reality
January 2000

Dimensions, portholes, worlds they spew from
their mouths. Cackles. Mocking. Laughter.
Bragging. Boasting. Claiming their character.
They separate, infiltrate, conjugate the distance
I feel. It's smothering, consuming, choking my
perception. How the creature longs to be one with
his Creator. I bleed. I fade. I crawl upon the floors
of my understanding. These mirrors of glimpses,
gazes, fragments ... only portray a resemblance of You.

Distorted. Distracted. Distraught over the faulty
images I see. You like a picture, a model, a painting.
I view You only as a reflection in the waters of my
limited revelation. Each pebble. Each stone. Each
rock of trial, of tension, of tragedy, only agitate my
once clear vision of You. The ripples remain distorting,
jolting, smearing my idol. Is it You I've been worshiping
or are these the ripples of my reality?

CHAPTER 7 =

LOVING GOD

"TO LOVE IS NOT A PART OF THINGS—OR A PART OF LIFE.
TO LOVE IS THE WHOLE OF THINGS—AND THE WHOLE OF LIFE."
—*Venus de Medici*[1]

REST STOP ON THE ROAD TO RELEVANCE

ON A journey, sometimes it's necessary to take a short rest stop. Thus, in
the beginning of chapters seven and eight, we'll do so. It's easy to get caught

up in the details and forget where we're headed. It's also easy to get lost in upcoming curves and turns in the road if we don't know they're coming. Therefore, review the crucial points before you continue on your journey.

For the sake of our discussion, it's insignificant how many parts you believe make up a person. What is significant is that you love God with all those parts in a holistic, interconnected fashion. If you love God in a partial or segmented fashion, you will be irrelevant. Many of us love God at times with our heart, at times with our soul, and at times with our mind, but few of us love God with our whole self all at once. Relevance is the unavoidable by-product of loving God in a holistic and interconnected fashion (when combined with loving your neighbor as yourself, which we'll study in chapter eight).

SIGNIFICANT PARTS

How many parts make up a person?

In the medical field, if you're referring to human bones, there are 206. If you're discussing how many muscles are in the human body, there are more than six hundred.[2]

In schools of religion, things get a little tricky. Theologians who believe man is one part support the model called monism.[3] Theologians who believe man is two parts—body and soul—support the model called dichotomy.[4] Theologians who believe man is three parts—body, soul, and spirit—support the model called trichotomy.[5]

Who really cares? When discussing the road to relevance, how is the number of parts that make up a man really significant?[6] I don't think Christ is so much concerned about how many parts make up a person, as much as He is about how a person views those parts in relationship to each other and what he or she does with those parts.[7]

"Teacher, which is the great commandment in the Law?"
And He said to him, "'You shall love the LORD your God with all your heart, and with all your soul, and with all your mind.'"
—Matthew 22:36-37

You would think that if this is the greatest commandment in all of the law, Jesus would have quoted Deuteronomy correctly and used the word "might," not "mind." As if this wasn't bad enough, the other Synoptic Gospels record Jesus affirming a seventh part of man.[8] In Mark and Luke, Jesus adds that man is to love God with all his strength, in addition to his heart, soul, and mind. If all the law and the prophets hang on this command to love God, then why are there several different lists of parts with which we are to love God? Why do Deuteronomy, Matthew, Mark, and Luke read differently? Either the specific parts or number of parts that make up a man are merely insignificant in this context, or is a deeper message being communicated?

LOVING GOD HOLISTICALLY

Science is only beginning to catch up to the brilliance of Jesus' teachings. I believe Christ knew something our generation is only starting to understand. Only in modern times have we come to see the importance of a mind-body connection.

Dating back to ancient Greece, philosophers viewed the world as being in conflict between the material and immaterial, the natural and the spiritual.[9] They compartmentalized these two entities, even labeling the material as bad. These two parts of a person were believed to be separate and distinct. "Centuries later, René Descartes, the great seventeenth century French mathematician and philosopher, reinforced this metaphysical divide in what came to be known in Western philosophy as mind-body dualism."[10]

Only recently, science and medicine are partnering to prove the Greeks and Descartes dead wrong. Man cannot be fragmented into different parts that are totally independent of one another. "Scientists are also learning something else," says Michael D. Lemonick. "Not only is the mind like the rest of the body, but the well-being of one is intimately intertwined with that of the other."[11]

Jesus spoke this truth thousands of years earlier. In fact, He understood the holistic interconnectedness of the mind-body-spirit since before the beginning of time. In His darkest hour, He didn't condemn the disciples when they forsook Him. He understood the link between the body and soul. He knew their physical weariness contributed to their spiritual weariness.

And He came to the disciples and found them sleeping, and said to Peter, "So, you men could not keep watch with Me for one hour? Keep watching and praying, that you may not enter into temptation; the spirit is willing, but the flesh is weak."
—Matthew 26:40-41

With this in mind, the command to love the Lord God with all our heart, soul, and mind makes perfect sense. It's no wonder God commanded holistic love. He knows us best, because He designed us. He knows that true love is holistic love.

I don't think God is concerned about how many parts we think comprise man. However, I do know He wants us to love Him with all those parts in an interconnected fashion. He knows if we love Him with only part of ourselves, we love Him incompletely. If we love Him incompletely, we have no hope of being relevant.

As we examine the content of Jesus' teachings, it's obvious He believed in the holistic interconnectedness of an individual. This is important for our study of relevance for one main reason: We can only be relevant when we love God in a holistic and interconnected manner. In other words, we must love God with all our heart, soul, and mind all at once.

This is why most us are irrelevant to God and the world around us. We love Him in a partial, segmented fashion that proves to be theologically incorrect and detrimental in our attempt at maintaining the life of a transformist. We love Him at times with our heart, at times with our soul, and at times with our mind, but most of us have no clue what it means to love God all those ways at once. We fail to love Him in a holistic interconnected manner. There are two main reasons why a partial segmented love for God is a flawed love.

Reason #1

A partial, segmented view of loving God is an offense to Him. This is the type of love characterized the Pharisees. They loved Him with their lips and their offerings, but not with their heart, soul, and mind. Their love for God was manufactured, insincere, and fragmented.

> *"You hypocrites, rightly did Isaiah prophesy of you, saying,*
> *'This people honors Me with their lips, But their heart is far away from Me.*
> *'But in vain do they worship Me, Teaching as doctrines the precepts of men.'"*
> —*Matthew 15:7-9*

Reason #2

A partial, segmented view of loving God makes us think we are better off than we really are. Jesus exposed the true sinful condition of mankind when He presented the need for holistic obedience and not just surface conformity. Most people can love God with a part of themselves. Anyone can look good on the outside. The true test is an all-encompassing love.

> *"You have heard that it was said, 'You shall not commit adultery';*
> *but I say to you, that everyone who looks on a woman to lust for her has committed*
> *adultery with her already in his heart."*
> —*Matthew 5:27-28*

If loving God was just about lip service, the Pharisees would have been the poster children. Unfortunately, Jesus said they were the ones farthest from the mark. In reality, the "real sinners," the prostitutes and tax collectors, were much closer to authentically loving God. What was their secret? What caused Jesus to be impressed with their love for Him?[12]

LOVING GOD WITH ALL YOUR HEART

If you surveyed the world, most people would tell you that intellectually, they believe there is a God. Surprisingly, many of these people would even claim to love that God. However, most of these "self proclaimed" God lovers love Him strictly with their heads. Sadly, they fail to love Him with their hearts.

Why? Why are so many people following in the footsteps of the

Pharisees? Why do the vast majority of people, inside and outside the Church, hide pockets of their hearts from God? Why do you and I fail to love God fully? Why do we prefer a dutiful religion that intellectually assents to a belief in God? Why are so few of us in a dangerous, adventurous, and passionate relationship with God? Why do guilt and fear characterize our faith when God longs for us to love Him with a fully engaged and reckless heart?

I believe there is one main reason for our half-hearted attempts. Loving God without our whole self is safer! If we're honest, we'd admit we're deathly afraid of what it would mean to love Him with our whole hearts. He's a dangerous lover.[13] He certainly cannot be controlled. So, we settle for a God who we can safely love with our heads.

We might throw a few dollars His direction. We might even attend a few religious services. Some of us may be extremely engaged in spiritual activities. But deep inside, we're deathly afraid. We appease Him with our works. We honor Him with our lips. But when it really comes down to it, who really wants to open his or her heart to a God who chose to let His own Son die? I mean right there, with that action, God clearly communicated that no one is immune to His crushing Hand, not even His own Son.

So, we turn up the radio. We turn down the prayer life. We work longer. We bury ourselves in our kids, our hobbies, the stock market, or anything else that can drown out the nagging pull that there is something more to our relationship with God.

We satisfy our empty hearts with food, things, achievements, sports, TV, and religion. We will give God our time, our talents, and our treasures. We will give Him everything—but our hearts. We willingly make ourselves slaves. We labor a lifetime to lay at His feet good works, when really all along, all He wants is our hearts.

Perhaps a segment of us have given up on this "good works" scene. We know we're wicked, so we live it up. We figure it's not worth the effort to please a God who's never pleased. So, we cut out our hearts and live purely for pleasure and self. We're not much different than the Pharisees in the first group.

Neither group of people lives or loves with their hearts. Instead, they're only shells and shadows of what they were intended to be.

Like Eve, we trust our own intuitions, and buy Satan's lie that God doesn't have our best interest in mind. We rely on our own preferences, assumptions, and calculations. We offer fragments of ourselves, hoping that as a result, we'll be on good terms with "the big guy upstairs."

This type of heartless love is really no love at all. It's centered in a fear-based religion. Realistically, it's not much different than animistic tribes that consume themselves with rituals in order to appease their gods. The true God wants more. He wants our hearts.

When we fail to love God with our hearts, it's because we fail to allow ourselves to become perfected in His love. We resist letting ourselves be loved. Did you catch it? We fail to love God with out hearts when we fail to let ourselves be loved. He extends His love to all of us, but few of us ever allow this process to take place. Strange, isn't it?

> *There is no fear in love; but perfect love casts out fear,*
> *because fear involves punishment, and the one who fears is not perfected in love.*
> *—1 John 4:18*

Why do you fail to let yourself be loved? Do you feel undeserving? Do you feel you're not really worth His love? At face value, this appears to be a humble approach, but in reality, it's laced with pride.[14] When we don't accept God's love because we feel unworthy, we're really putting ourselves in a position where we think we know better than God does. Of course we're unworthy! Nonetheless, God loves us! To reject His offer of love is to pursue a way that seems right to us, but in the end only leads to death.[15]

Why do you fail to let yourself be loved? Is it because you are ticked off at God? Has He allowed some form of evil to befall you? Has He allowed you to be abused, abandoned, or alone? Has He permitted an injustice to take place? Have you allowed fear to replace a simple faith? Does this evil permeate your thinking, rather than His love? This type of thinking, when unchecked, can be toxic to your faith. God is bigger than our anger. He's not put off by our emotions of rage. Instead, He asks us to share our anger with Him.[16] He invites us into relationship.

For some of us, our own sense of unworthiness and anger may deter us from loving God with our hearts. However, the most common cause of heartless love is that partial love allows safety.

God is a wild lover. To love Him with our hearts would be to release control. Such a love leads us into uncharted waters and unexamined paths. It's paved with risk and adventure. It's unsafe.

C.S. Lewis, in one of his books from the Chronicles of Narnia, *The Lion, the Witch, and the Wardrobe*, brilliantly captures the fear that defines our human condition. He expounds upon the fact that God is unsafe. Lewis cleverly demonstrates this through Lucy and Susan's conversation with Mr. and Mrs. Beaver about Aslan the lion. They have yet to meet Him and reveal in their dialogue a bit of the apprehension they feel concerning a personal encounter with this King.

"Is he a man?" asked Lucy.

"Aslan a man!" said Mr. Beaver sternly. "Certainly not. I tell you he is the King of the wood and son of the great Emperor-Beyond-the-Sea. Don't you know who is the King of the Beasts? Aslan is a lion—the lion, the great Lion."

"Ooh!" said Susan, "I'd thought he was a man. Is he quite safe? I shall feel rather nervous about meeting a lion."

"That you will, dearie, and no mistake," said Mrs. Beaver, "if there's anyone who can appear before Aslan without their knees knocking, they're either braver than most or just else silly."

"Then he isn't safe?" said Lucy.

"Safe?" said Mr. Beaver; "don't you hear what Mrs. Beaver tells you? Who said anything about safe? 'Course he isn't safe. But he's good. He's the King I tell you."

I believe we're all nervous to meet the King in a relationship where our hearts are unguarded. It's too unsafe. Perhaps this is why most of the world rejects the offensive emasculated god we present. They know better!

You and I present a god who is manageable, controllable, and merely benevolent. We've shunned introducing a God who is wild, unsafe, and good, because we ourselves have shunned this God.

We can't fake loving with our hearts. No one can. So, we settle for loving God with our heads or our hands. We offer a partial, segmented love and in affect, fail to love Him holistically.

Relevance is merely the unavoidable by-product of a holistic interconnected love for God and people. How do we love Him with all our hearts? We need to meet God. We need to get into the presence of the King, not the pitiful idols we erect, regardless if He's unsafe. He is good!

> WE CAN'T FAKE LOVING WITH OUR HEARTS. NO ONE CAN. SO, WE SETTLE FOR LOVING GOD WITH OUR HEADS OR OUR HANDS.

To love anything less is to settle for a cheap imitation. In a few moments, we'll find out more about cheap imitations. But for now, understand that an imitation is a cancer of the heart. To love Him with less than our whole hearts is to be consumed with irrelevance.

LOVING GOD WITH ALL YOUR SOUL

Bill and Jenny were well over the honeymoon stage of their marriage. After ten years and two kids, they wondered what had gone wrong. There were no longer any burning embers in their relationship, certainly no nights of passion or intimacy. Instead, it seemed as though their marriage was a contract whereby they carried out duties of heartless service.

The days of wonder, adventure, and spontaneity had fizzled out years earlier. Bill was consumed with his job and golf hobby. Jenny spent much of her time living her life through the kids. She found out her three-year-old could carry on a deeper conversation than Bill. Bitterness and sarcasm dripped from her every word and her every action. Bill and Jenny, once proclaimed soul mates, now no longer knew the first thing about each other's souls. This beautiful relationship turned sour and was only a hollow shell of what it once was.

Does this paint a pretty good picture of your relationship with God? Have you lost your first love? Has the passion and intimacy been replaced with duty and heartless service? Has the wonder and adventure gone by the wayside? Have you moved from loving God with all your soul to barely liking Him with your lip service?

If Bill and Jenny ever hope to return to an intimate, fulfilling relationship, certain things must change. They must move beyond loving each other with strictly lip service. They must stop living and loving with their heads and return to loving each other with their souls.

What's the solution for you and I? If we want to be relevant—and being relevant means loving God with all our souls—then how do we rekindle those long-smoldering embers? What can jump-start a dying relationship again?

Two groups of people are truly alive in this world. The first group is comprised of those who have had a near-death experience. Think for a moment. If you want to talk about a fired-up person, look at someone who has been in a very bad accident, someone who has recovered from a terminal illness, someone who has experienced a brush with death. That person lives life with purpose. She is pumped up. She is fired up. She knows what she's been saved from. She doesn't waste any time with explanations or apologies.

The second group of people is made up of brand new Christians. When I say brand new Christians, I mean those who were really down and out. Of course we're all sinners, but do you know what I mean when I say the down and out? I'm talking about the heroin addict who beat his sister and robbed his mother for his last high. I'm talking about the girl crippled with low self-esteem and as a result is addicted to cutting her arms as a release from pain. I'm talking about the man who has been deeply entrenched in a works-oriented religiosity in an attempt to earn favor with God.

When these people come to find life in Christ, they are radically empowered and impassioned to live out their faith without any regret. They are supernaturally charged. They have all five senses alive and are in tune with the world.

So what about us? What are we supposed to do? How do we come alive? Are we just simply supposed to be placed upon the shelf of irrelevancy? What about when real life hits? How can we remain in a state of loving God with all our souls?

It is my conviction that we stop loving God with all our souls when we stop seeing God for who He is. There are other religions out there that actually believe "as man now is God once was, as God now is man may become."[17] In other words, God is only a little bit higher up on the food chain than us, and if we play our cards right, we can soon be at His level.

> **WE HAVE LOST A HIGH VIEW OF GOD. WE TRY TO MAKE HIM SO PALATABLE TO THE WORLD AROUND THAT HE SIMPLY LOSES HIS APPEAL.**

I've never endorsed this belief, but there have been times when I lived my life as if I did. For many of us, there is no awe of God. We have lost a high view of God. We try to make Him so palatable to the world around that He simply loses His appeal. He is our pocket Jesus, our God in a box.

Look for a second at the people who really grasped intimacy with God—the "super saints" who loved God with all their souls. What was their secret?

SEEING OUR SIN

In the year of King Uzziah's death, I saw the Lord sitting on a throne, lofty and exalted, with the train of His robe filling the temple. Seraphim stood above Him, each having six wings; with two he covered his face, and with two he covered his feet, and with two he flew. And one called out to another and said, "Holy, Holy, Holy, is the LORD of hosts, The whole earth is full of His glory." And the foundations of the thresholds trembled at the voice of him who called out, while the temple was filling with smoke. Then I said, "Woe is me, for I am ruined! Because I am a man of unclean lips, And I live among a people of unclean lips;
For my eyes have seen the King, the LORD of hosts."
—Isaiah 6:1-5

Talk about a guy who had a high view of God! As he became intimately acquainted with the God of the universe, Isaiah very quickly realized the sinfulness and depravity that consumed his heart. As he saw the raw holiness of God, Isaiah immediately realized his own sinful condition.

But this was in the Old Testament though. That was so long ago. Is there a New Testament example of someone who was intimate with God? More importantly, if there is an example, how was this person motivated to love God with all his or her soul?

And behold, there was a woman in the city who was a sinner; and when she learned that He was reclining at the table in the Pharisee's house, she brought an alabaster vial of perfume, and standing behind Him at His feet, weeping, she began to wet His feet with her tears, and kept wiping them with the hair of her head, and kissing His feet, and anointing them with the perfume.
—Luke 7:37-38

This woman didn't need anyone to tell her of her sinful condition. The moment she encountered Jesus, an internal love birthed that would not rest until it could be visually demonstrated. There was no shame. There were no apologies.

We see the demonstration of her love, but what caused her to love God with all her soul? What allowed her to have a fresh and vibrant love that moved her to authentic action?

"For this reason I say to you, her sins, which are many, have been forgiven, for she loved much; but he who is forgiven little, loves little."
—Luke 7:47

She loved much because she sinned a lot? Does that mean that I have to sin a whole bunch to love God a whole bunch? If that's true, the Bible seems to contradict itself.

The depth of our love is not based on how much we sin, but rather on how much we know we sin. This knowledge can only be understood when in the presence of something or someone who is not sin ...God Himself.

So many times we compare ourselves to the real "big sinners." We rationalize that we're not as bad as "so and so." The only problem is that "so and so" is not the standard of holiness. God is. When we start to feel our love for God growing cold, it's probably because we've not been intimate with Him in a while.

Perhaps the reason our love for God is low is because our intimacy with God is low. The result of not seeing Him is that we don't see His holiness. Without a standard of holiness to compare ourselves against, we look pretty good. As a result, we think we're better off than we really are. There is no need for gratitude because, in our minds, there is no need for grace.

Do you want to be relevant with the world around you? Do you want to be like one of those people who have had a near-death experience? Do you desire to be truly alive? If so, then understand the fact that you've already had a near-death experience, spiritually speaking. The flames of hell were gripping you at your heels. You and I both deserve eternal punishment because of our offensive sin toward a holy God. Comprehending this will propel you into loving God with all your soul.

I'm talking about having a one-on-one encounter with the God of the universe. I'm referring to becoming intimately acquainted with the God who is so otherworldly that just a glimpse of His Word causes your bones to break.

> *I heard and my inward parts trembled, At the sound my lips quivered.*
> *Decay enters my bones, And in my place I tremble ...*
> *—Habakkuk 3:16*

Have you ever been around new Christians who are fired up because they know what they have been saved from? Do you remember the strange but exciting vibes given off by someone who is intimately acquainted with his or her sinful condition? Get into the presence of God, and you'll see your condition for who and what it really is. Most likely when you truly come to grips with what you have been forgiven from, you will have an authentic ability to love God with all your soul.

With a smile, I think back to Sunday school. Those plastic chairs, the paste, the crayons, and of course, the flannel graph, all conjure up images of pleasure and wonder. I remember at the time, I didn't really care too much about the Second Commandment. Somehow, for a five-year-old, the prohibition "you shall not make for yourself an idol" really didn't matter too much. In fact, the motive or pay off of bowing down and worshiping a golden calf really didn't click with me. I remember thinking the Israelites must have been really dumb.

It was not until years later, when I read *The Knowledge of the Holy*, that I truly understood the grotesque idols that captured the affections of my own mind. A.W. Tozer wrote, "The idolatrous heart assumes that God is other than He is—in itself a monstrous sin—and substitutes for the true God one made after its own likeness. The essence of idolatry is the entertainment of thoughts about God that are unworthy of Him."

I was immediately convicted. How many times have I approached God on my terms? How many times have I made subtle bargains with the idol I've made? How many times have I taken God Almighty and mixed Him with my desires, my wishes, and my dreams, and formed a god that is an utter offense to the true God? How many times have I fashioned an object of worship that does not even represent an accurate picture of the Creator of the universe?

I believe author Michael S. Horton sheds some light on how many of us erect idols in our own minds. Curiously, this often happens through Christian media.

> Music—and art in general—should not be forced to always serve a cerebral, intellectual objective that is associated with preaching or reading Scripture or a book of theology. There is nothing wrong with art appealing primarily to the feeling and imagination, but there is a great deal wrong with worship that is motivated by feelings and imagination. Therefore, church music

should be judged by criteria that are very different from those by which we judge common art. There is nothing unspiritual about enjoying a secular concert simply to be entertained. While we should not be naïve about the worldviews that shape secular music or ignore the lyrics because we like the music, we do not have to be rigorously analytical about the music. But we must be rigorously analytical about sacred music. Why? Because it is used not in our own entertainment but in the Worship of God!

In the Old Testament, when people worshiped God on their own terms, in their own ways, it meant judgment, death, and discipline. This process is seen in Cain's offering, Nadab's strange fire, and Saul's sacrifice.[18] With regard to worship, each example illustrates how men thought they could come to God on their own terms. God did not view these as misunderstandings, but rather idolatrous attempts that elevated worship to a higher level than God Himself. Remember, God stated in black and white, "You shall not make for yourselves other gods before me."[19]

Suddenly, the Israelites don't look that dumb. Before we even talk about loving God with our minds, we need to first tear down the idols we have erected in our own lives. These shadows of God are not God at all! To worship God in a manner devoid of truth is to worship an idol.

Tozer continues, "If we insist upon trying to imagine Him, we end up with an idol, made not with hands, but with thoughts; and an idol of the mind is as offensive to God as an idol of the hand. Left to ourselves, we tend immediately to reduce God to manageable terms. We want a god we can control. We need the feeling of security that comes from knowing what God is like."

What are some of the idols we've created within our own minds? There are many. I encourage you to examine yourself. Getting a true picture of God will naturally reveal the counterfeits that reside in your head. These idols of the mind need to be torn down if we ever hope to be relevant. Loving an idol breeds irrelevance.

For the time being, I will only touch on one idol. There are thousands that fight to occupy our hearts. However, I believe most of these are symptomatic to the one I will now mention. I believe one of the fundamental idols our generation has erected is that of a Lordless salvation.

So many people accept Jesus as Savior and not as Lord. Peter struggled with this. He wanted Jesus to fit his mold. Peter wanted Jesus only to have limited control in his life. In fact, three times Peter told Jesus, "No, Lord."[20] This is an oxymoron. If Jesus is your Savior, then He has permission as Lord to any part of your life. You can't say "no" to Him.

Many of us believe we can add Jesus Christ to our lives. In other words, we get our fire insurance from the flames of hell and then never move on in our growth. We see Jesus merely as a rescue boat from the sea of sin. Sadly, we never allow Jesus to be the Lord that He is when it comes to our personal lives. Most of us go on living according to our own standards, our own desires, and our own wishes.

As I examine the Scriptures, I don't see this as a viable option. Hear me out—I don't believe for a second we can add an ounce of anything to our salvation; this is blasphemous and a cancer to the mind. It's not because we make Jesus Lord that we obtain salvation. However, as I search the New Testament, I never see Jesus presenting Himself as something we merely add to our lives, along with a bunch of other things. He never told people to accept Him and just do what they want. He told them point blank, "Follow Me."[21]

He does come as Savior, but He also comes as Lord. The message is similar to two sides of the same coin. He never permitted His followers to add Him to their lives. We don't come to Christ on our own terms.

DON'T LET YOUR NETS BECOME ANCHORS

Often, we gloss over the initial call ("follow Me") to discipleship that Peter, Andrew, James, and John experienced. Remember, by trade, each was a fisherman. This was not a job for "the weak or indolent."[22] Fishermen were crude in manner, rough in speech and in their treatment of others.[23] Fishing was a very prominent and secure industry in that day.[24] The great demand for fresh fish allowed cities to be centered around this industry.[25]

Jesus' imperative consisted of two words: "Follow Me!"[26] At best, He promised them a confusing alternative instead of fishing for fish.[27] His guarantee of making them fishers of men wasn't all that attractive.[28] Obviously in retrospect, this call somewhat refers to the Great Commission in Matthew 28. However, the twelve probably had no idea initially what this meant.

> **WE DON'T COME TO CHRIST ON OUR OWN TERMS.**

It's very easy to think of fishing as a business that Peter and friends were crawling to get out of.[29] The words, "immediately they left their nets and followed him," seem pretty trivial when separated from the emotion behind their actions.[30] Their nets were means of financial provision, security, familiarity, and identity.[31] Besides this, some even had families to provide for.[32] Peter later reiterates the fact that he and others left everything to follow Christ.[33] There were no means of contemplation or reference of rationalizing.[34] When Christ called them, the disciples abandoned "good things" for a greater goal.[35] Their nets (natural talents, means of financial gain, identity, significance) did not become anchors, holding them back from moving into a deeper relationship with God.

Matthew also responded promptly when the Lord called him with the words, "Follow Me."[36] Matthew was at his place of employment. The nets he gave up were financial security, identity, and livelihood. Matthew may have given up earthly riches, but he gained heavenly reward. The first step was reckless abandonment. You can't go with God and stay with self.

True discipleship does not mean heartless devotion and needless sacrifice. However, in modern day, the Church has bought a lie on the other extreme. This falsehood permeates society as a whole as well. This philosophy is the "name-it-claim-it, God exists to bless you" doctrine. The Church has fallen asleep in comfort and ease. Apathy has been the most violent killer of passion for Christ. Materialism has whispered its silent kiss of death upon ignorant Christians.

Presently, Christ calls people to follow Him. Sadly, many of us just appear to want a ticket out of hell. We want to skip over the Lordship, the "loving God with our whole self" part. In a symbolic sense, many Christians have allowed their nets (natural talents, identity, jobs, security) to become anchors, holding them back from a deeper knowledge of Christ. "Immediately" Peter, James, John, and Andrew released their nets, those good things God had given them, for a greater cause.[37] They did not permit cares of the world or desires for financial security to weigh them down from following their Master.

Hebrews 12:1 speaks about these "nets" as even potentially good things.[38] These things are not sinful habits, lifestyles, or activities. Discipleship not only demands the abandonment of sin, but also good things that take precedent and priority over the love relationship with God. These things entangle us. Paul even considered his righteousness, education, descent, and confidence as refuse compared to knowing Christ.[39] This is the crux of holistic love, the stripping away of all idols that may rob your devotion from the Lord.

What are the imitations that have captured your mind? What are those idols you clutch so tightly? What would it take for you to release those into your Father's hands?

No verse in Scripture promises we'll always receive abundant material blessings in return for giving up things in God's name. Some disciples will never see their reward here on earth. God did reward Abraham's faith when he demonstrated he would sacrifice Isaac.[40] Jesus did promise Peter he will rule with Him over the twelve tribes of Israel.[41] Believers today are promised that "everyone who has left houses or brothers or sisters or father or mother or children or fields for my sake will receive a hundred times as much and will inherit eternal life."

However, sometimes things may look bleak. In Hebrews 11, some saw the dead raised, seas parted, and walls fall. Others were sawn in two or afflicted. In the final accounting, at the end of time, true disciples will receive rewards that are unfathomable.

What are the nets in your life? In other words, what are those "good things" God has given you that crowd Him out of your heart? For me at times, some of my "nets" have been relationships, dreams, and hobbies. In and of themselves, these things weren't bad or harmful. In fact, most of these items were tools God used to eventually deepen my relationship with Him. However, if left unchecked, these "nets" can quickly become the things "which so easily entangle" my heart. These nets can become anchors that weigh down my relationship with God.

Once the Spirit identifies your anchors, you have a choice. You can reject the conviction, or you can remove the anchors with His power.

> **GOD WILL REVEAL HIMSELF AS WE DEVOTE OURSELVES TO PRAYER, INTENSIVE STUDY OF HIS WORD, AND OBEDIENCE.**

Those objects contribute to the idols of the mind that we erect. Once torn down, we can begin to love God in a holistic and interconnected manner.

How do we remove these idols? We don't; God does. God will reveal Himself as we devote ourselves to prayer, intensive study of His Word, and obedience. Isn't this what He wrote?

"Whoever has my commands and obeys them, he is the one who loves me. He who loves me will be loved by my Father, and I too will love him and show myself to him."
—John 14:21

In simple terms, when we obey God, He inevitably shows up. So, as we act in faith to what He's written, in exchange, He'll manifest Himself. As He reveals Himself, obviously we're made aware of the idols we've erected. As we tear down these idols, in the power of His strength, a proper perspective of God remains. Then, and only then, can we truly begin to love God, the true God, with all our minds.

THE EXAMPLE IN OZ

The greatest command is to love God with our hearts, souls, and minds. When we fail to love Him in this way, we're incomplete. Ironically, there were three famous figures in *The Wizard of OZ* who also felt incomplete.

The tin man lacked a heart. The lion lacked courage (a soul). The Scarecrow lacked a brain (a mind). They all recognized their incompleteness, and they too went on a journey to have an experience with the only one who could give them what they lacked.

We walk the road to relevance. They traveled the yellow brick road. Both paths contain surprises. Some are bright, and some are dark.

We're far from a transformed mind, but this chapter covered some major ground. Half the battle of being relevant is loving God. It can't be avoided. But it's not our final destination. Relevance is also about loving people.

> *Beloved, if God so loved us, we also ought to love one another.*
> *—1 John 4:11*

MY JOURNAL IN THE JOURNEY

Valjean
November 1999

Given a name, running from it an entire lifetime
Received a sentence, my justification a debtor's plea
Wasted a gift, knowing only rules and regulations
Died a season, slavery the familiar breath of pride

Destroyed a promise, finding such solace in chains
Removing a hope, thrusting the last doubt into my heart
Choking a dream, convinced myself this is all there is
Embracing a punishment, fleeing from who I really am

Stayed a prisoner, asceticism a frequent visitor
Knew a key, existed beyond my obvious failures
Believed a lie, held that gun to my box of religion
Sold a vision, convinced myself I exhausted the options

Experienced a mystery, couldn't accept what was already free
Witnessed a paradox, shouldn't define what's beyond words
Perceived a yoke, part of me died on that day
Cherished a pardon, given, a purpose instead

Confounded a man, who never knew he was bound
Freed a captive, my chains were self-made rules
Taught a teacher, my lectures became personal reality
Saved a wretch, can't be called a servant, you've made me a son

CHAPTER 8=
LOVING PEOPLE

> "THE ONLY FEELING OF REAL LOSS IS WHEN YOU LOVE
> SOMEONE MORE THAN YOU LOVE YOURSELF."
> —*From the film* Good Will Hunting

REST STOP ON THE ROAD TO RELEVANCE

JUST LIKE we pulled over for a rest stop in the beginning of chapter
seven, we need to do so again. This chapter has even more curves and turns

in the road. It's easy to get lost if we don't know what's coming. Therefore, review the crucial points below before you continue on your journey.

Relevance is maintained by loving God (holistically and interconnected), as well as loving your neighbor as yourself.

Most of us love ourselves in the wrong way.

This "self-love" is twisted, wrapped with layers of self-hatred and pride.

We all naturally struggle with destructive thoughts and actions (whether personally manifested in shopaholism, churchaholism, alcoholism, etc.) that feed the downward spiral of loving ourselves the wrong way.

The result of loving ourselves the wrong way is that we cannot love others the right way, and thus we are irrelevant.

The solution to being relevant is to love ourselves the right way, the way God loves us.

In order to understand the way God loves us, we need to realize the difference between our condition (how we are on earth) and our position (who we are in Christ).

Truly understanding our position will allow us to love ourselves the right way, the way God does.

Loving ourselves the right way will allow us to love others the right way and thus be relevant.

LOVING YOURSELF

Strange as it may seem, we can't move one step further on the road to relevance unless we first love ourselves. You may find that odd or heretical.

There has been a tremendous surge of interest in self-help books and over-the-counter pop psychology offered at local bookstores. Such "medication" comes in many shapes and sizes. Regardless, the most common theme seems to be the idea that people need to love themselves.

Is this contrary to Christ's message of denying self? How can we love ourselves and at the same time deny ourselves? Was Christ wrong to assume people naturally love themselves? After all, He said the second greatest commandment, the other half of being relevant, is to "love your neighbor as yourself." How can we love others if we don't love ourselves?

As I look at the world today, I see a world that hates itself. "Hate" is a very strong word. Maybe a better phrase is that people fail to love themselves the right way. Ironically, I believe that loving ourselves the wrong way will foster a deep internal self-hatred. How is this so? Just look at the self-destructive habits with which much of the world, including Christians, struggle. Cutters, drug abusers, alcoholics, shopaholics, workaholics, churchaholics, and people who suffer from anorexia or bulimia make up the broken world in which we live.

WE CAN'T MOVE ONE STEP FURTHER ON THE ROAD TO RELEVANCE UNLESS WE FIRST LOVE OURSELVES.

Look at Church history. Throughout the centuries, many self-proclaimed followers of Christ willingly underwent self-inflicted physical pain. The official name given this practice is asceticism. Many have viewed asceticism as a way to express sorrow or penance for sin. Self-flagellation was an attempted means of "paying" for sin. People felt so much hatred for their evil habits that the only way to visually communicate that hatred was self-directed pain.

Although these are extreme examples, they all relate to a similar problem that will most certainly prevent us from loving others and thus being relevant. Think about the addictions and disorders listed above. What do anorexia, bulimia, shopaholism, churchaholism, workaholism, alcoholism, drug abuse, cutting, and asceticism all have in common? They are all ways meant to help us cope with pain. They are actions and thinking patterns intended to fill a void, a deep emptiness, within us all.

I believe God looks with sorrow upon cutters, alcoholics, and any other person who attempts to fill the void on his or her own. He longs so much to fill the void which sin creates. He longs to quench the thirst that only living water can satisfy.[1]

Modern day self-help books do an excellent job at diagnosing and revealing pain and disorders. However, the solutions they offer to fill the void are often just as empty as the void itself. We need the medicine the Creator has provided. After all, wouldn't the only One who's allowed the void be the only One who can ultimately fill the void?

The problem is not that we don't love ourselves enough. Even though we're a society that hates itself, anyone can see that we're also a society that is utterly consumed with self. "It is out of self-love that all our other evil passions spring," writes the great Scottish preacher Alexander Whyte.[2] "The whole fall and ruin and misery of our present human nature lies in this, that in every human being self-love has taken, in addition to its own place, the place of the love of God and of the love of man also. We naturally now love nothing and no one but ourselves."

Although asceticism, at first glance, seems to be extremely pious, in reality it's an action that's wrapped in a twisted form of self-love and self-hatred. When followers of Christ reenacted forms of self-punishment as a penance for sin, they communicated with their actions that Christ's payment on the cross was not sufficient payment for their sin. As a result, they needed to mix in their own efforts to gain redemption.

People are extremely creative in compensating for their internal void. Sadly, many teens prostitute their bodies, abuse their minds with drugs, and deny their pain with compulsive addictions like shopping and gambling. Many young males are caught up in an alternative reality fleshed out in need to always play video games. Choose your "drug." Humanity is addicted to silencing the emptiness with whatever means available.

As we're beginning to see, the sticking point is not that we fail to love ourselves, but that we fail to love ourselves the right way. We fail to love ourselves the way God loves us.

Self-esteem refers to the way we think and feel about ourselves. People with low self-esteem naturally have a poor self-image. They don't think about themselves with a healthy perspective.

Ironically, their thought pattern is closely related to a biblical worldview. The Bible doesn't say many things that should boost our self-esteem. It says that our attempts at righteousness are as filthy rags.[3] It states that no good thing dwells in us.[4] We are like sheep that have turned away and gone after our own way.[5] There is a way that seems right to us, but in the end it kills.[6]

If you still have high self-esteem, just keep reading the passage in Romans. It's obvious God sees us differently than the way pop psychology tells us we should see ourselves.

As it is written, "There is none righteous, not even one; There is none who understands, There is none who seeks for God; All have turned aside, together they have become useless; There is none who does good, There is not even one. Their throat is an open grave, With their tongues they keep deceiving, The poison of asps is under their lips; Whose mouth is full of cursing and bitterness; Their feet are swift to shed blood, Destruction and misery are in their paths, And the path of peace have they not known. There is no fear of God before their eyes." —Romans 3:10-18

If the Bible is so "negative" about the human heart, how will this help us to love ourselves the right way? We've only looked at half of the story so far. The reality is that even though all those things mentioned above are true about us, the Bible also says many positive things as well.

TERMS OF THE TRADE

I believe there is a lot of confusion in the Church today about self-esteem. Some people think God views us as depraved sinners. Others believe God views us as holy and perfect. The truth is, the Bible says both.

We need to realize the difference between our condition and our position. Our condition is how we are. In other words, our condition is the way we behave, act, and think. Our position is who we are. In other words, our position is the standing, privilege, and status we are because of Christ.

Failure to distinguish the difference between these two terms and how God views us concerning them may contribute to a low self-esteem. It can foster feelings of self-hatred, disgust, and depression. On the contrary, a healthy and clear understanding of these terms and what they mean can foster feelings of proper self-love. The life change happens when we understand how these terms relate with one another and how God views us after Christ's righteousness is imparted to us.

CONDITION		POSITION	
HOW I AM	Romans 7:19-21	WHO I AM	Eph. 1:4, 18
OLD MAN	Gal. 5:24, Rom. 6.6	NEW MAN	Rom. 6:4, 22
TEMPORAL	2 Cor. 4:18	ETERNAL	2 Cor. 4:18
SEEN	2 Cor 4:18	UNSEEN	2 Cor. 4:18
PHYSICAL	Romans 7:18	SPIRITUAL	1 Cor. 1:2
FALSE SELF	Romans 7:17	TRUE SELF	2 Cor. 5:17
OUTER MAN	2 Cor. 4:16	INNER MAN	2 Cor. 4:16

Figure 8.1 - Condition vs. Postion

A LITTLE ABOUT CONDITION

The moment we get a true glimpse of God, we realize we're utterly depraved and sinful in our condition. In other words, according to our definition, how we are is sinful. That will never change completely until death or the rapture. There is a false teaching out there that says we can eradicate sin completely this side of heaven. In truth, we'll always have the presence of sin until we are glorified.

Nevertheless, God expects us to sin less. We are told to live holy.[7] We are able to live holy. God has freely given us all things so that we can be equipped to do every good work.[8]

So why do we sin? Why are most of our lives consumed with sin? Why is loving people often the farthest thing from our minds?

We fail to love people because we fail to live in light of our position. Heck, most of us don't even know our position in Christ. Remember that our condition is how we are, and our position is who we are. There is a big difference. Yet I believe that the secret to being holy in our condition is to live in light of our position.

YOU'RE NOT READY YET

How many times have you heard, "They shouldn't get married yet? They're too young. They don't even know who they are." Whether through a sitcom, a counseling situation, or a passing conversation, I've heard so many people use phrases like these. "Marriage is a big step; you shouldn't enter down that road if you don't know who you are."

Strangely, there is a lot of truth to that statement, especially in terms of being relevant. My advice to you is, relevance is a big step; you shouldn't enter down that road if you don't know who you are!

THE SECRET TO BEING HOLY IN OUR CONDITION IS TO LIVE IN LIGHT OF OUR POSITION.

So if you're a believer, who are you? What is your position in Christ? Here are just a handful of things that are true about you. You are: accepted in the Beloved (Ephesians 2:6), bought with a price (1 Corinthians 6:20), crucified with Christ (Galatians 2:20), dwelt by the Holy Spirit (1 Corinthians 3:16), enslaved to God (Romans 6:22), freed from slavery to sin (Romans 6:18), God's child (Romans 8:14), heir of God's riches (Galatians 4:6-7), in Him complete (Colossians 2:10), Jesus' chosen inheritance (Ephesians 1:4), kingly priest (1 Peter 2:9), light of the world (Matthew 5:14), mastered no longer by sin (Romans 6:14), new creation (2 Corinthians 5:14), one spirit with the Lord (1 Corinthians 6:17), perfect in Christ (Hebrews 10:14), quieted in the reality of who God is (Psalm 46:10), raised up with Him (Ephesians 2:5-6), seated in heavenly places with Christ (Ephesians 2:5-6), transformed into the image of Christ (2 Corinthians 3:18), united to the Lord (1 Corinthians 6:17), victorious through my Lord (1 Corinthians 15:57), wonderfully made (Psalm 139:14), workmanship (Ephesians 2:10), yoked with righteousness (2 Corinthians 6:14), zealous of good works (Titus 2:14).

There is so much here in these positional truths. It's easy to zip right through them. The reality is, if you've trusted Christ Jesus as your Lord and Savior, in that moment, each of the statements above are true about you whether you feel like it or not. You don't have to wait until you reach heaven for them to be true. These positional truths are not dependent upon a sinful past, feelings, performance, time, space, or anything else. They are true because God said they are, and in Him there is no untruth.[9]

HOW RELEVANCE RELATES

After you're justified, God no longer views you as anything less than perfect because of the blood of Christ. You're fully accepted as the beloved. You no longer have to try to earn, perform, or maintain pleasure with Him. If you've truly been saved, nothing you do can separate you from the love of God.[10]

We've covered a lot of ground in this chapter. We've talked about how we need to love people in order to be relevant. Christ said we need to love others as ourselves. We've learned that most of us have a twisted and unhealthy form of love for ourselves. This "love" is wrapped in layers of self-hatred. This self-hatred expresses itself in many destructive habits, such as self-mutilation, churchaholism, workaholism, alcoholism, shopaholism, anorexia, bulimia, and many, many, others.

When we focus merely on our condition, we remain in a state of self-hatred. We'll naturally realize our condition when we're in the presence of a holy God. As Paul grew closer to God, as his sanctification increased, he saw with each passing day, more and more, how utterly sinful his condition was without the righteousness of Christ.

Interestingly, Paul described his condition to his readers. Chronologically, Paul first labeled himself as the "least of the apostles" (1 Corinthians 15:9). As he lived longer he began to see that "how he was" turned out to be worse than he first imagined. Therefore, he labeled himself as the "least of all saints" (Ephesians 3:8). Ironically, in one of his latter letters comparatively speaking, Paul penned some very shocking words as a commentary on his condition. Paul said that he was the "chief of all sinners" (1 Timothy 1:15).

Paul understood the intricacies of his condition. But he didn't stop here. He balanced the understanding of his condition in the backdrop of his position. Paul, more than anyone else, a former persecutor of the Church, realized he was a new creation in Christ![11] And just like Paul, our condition we will be transformed if we live in light of our position.

As we allow God to teach us about who we are in Christ, we'll be able to stop viewing people as competition or threat to our esteem. If we view others as a threat to our esteem, we'll by no means be able to love or serve them.

HAVING THE RUBBER HIT THE ROAD

What event, besides His death on the cross, best depicted Jesus' love for mankind? Was it when He released the woman caught in adultery from condemnation? Was it when He raised Lazarus from the dead?

The event that depicted his love for people, just as good as any other, was when He washed the disciples' feet. Most of us fail to recognize the thought process prior to His action of love. Within this lies the secret to loving people.

Jesus, knowing that the Father had given all things into His hands, and that He had come forth from God, and was going back to God ... —John 13:3

Jesus, our model and forerunner, gave us an example that we would do well to follow.[12] Immediately, before taking the towel, Jesus reflected back to all God had given Him, where He had come from, and where He was going. Jesus thought upon who He was. He focused on His position! And what did this cause Him to do? Jesus ...

... rose from supper, and laid aside His garments; and taking a towel, He girded Himself about. Then He poured water into the basin, and began to wash the disciples' feet, and to wipe them with the towel with which He was girded. —John 13:4-5

The disciples couldn't take on the form of a servant and wash each other's feet. They couldn't do the loving thing because they were focused upon proving their position, in an earthly sense. In their minds, their position was an unsettled reality. In fact, Jesus rebuked them many times for arguing who was the greatest.[13] Jesus, unlike the disciples, knew His position was secure. He could lower himself to love and serve because He didn't have to prove anything.

Did you catch it? The secret to loving others is realizing our position is secure. Only a secure person who knows his position in Christ can lower himself and love others.

We can only love others when we're not focusing on ourselves. We can only focus on others when we truly grasp our position in Christ. When we understand who we are in Christ, we can love ourselves as God loves us, in a manner that is biblically accurate.

We must love others. As Philo of Alexandria uttered in the fifth century, "Be kind, for everyone you meet is fighting a great battle." A key in loving others is to love ourselves. As we've learned though, this is much different than the world's understanding of self-love. The people most loving in life are those who don't have to prove who they are. Rather, they already know who they are.

John Eldredge, in his book *Wild at Heart*, provides amazing insight:[14]

> Too many Christians today are living back in the old covenant.[15] They believe that their heart is desperately wicked. NOT SO![16] Your flesh is not you. It is not the real you. My sin is not me. It is not my true heart. You are a lot more than a sinner saved by grace. You are a new creation in Christ. You are a saint, called one. The real side of you is on the side of God against the false self. The man who wants to live valiantly will lose heart quickly if he believes that his heart is nothing but sin. Why fight? The battle feels lost before it even begins. Your flesh is your false self. The only way to deal with it is to crucify it. We are never told to crucify our heart. We are never told to get rid of those deep desires for battle and beauty and adventure. We are told to shoot the traitor.

Moreover, I will give you a new heart and put a new spirit within you. —Ezekiel 36:26

MY JOURNAL IN THE JOURNEY

In
November 1999

I break from clarity for just a moment in time.
I flee organized thoughts in search of a deeper
realm. I step outside my box for an instant of
uncalculated experience. I strive that I may be
at peace, for a forgotten break in time.

In that threshold of understanding. In that
second of unconscious remembrance. In that
advent of comprehension. In that unstable
source of peace.

I am fully known and not rejected. I am accepted
and understood. I am at rest within my laboring.
I embrace your mind as we enter this reality.

In this red pill ignorance fades. In this space the
lines aren't defined. In this dream we can't
maintain it. In you I never want to get out.

CHAPTER 9

BALANCING FAITH

INTEGRATION INTO EVERYDAY LIFE

"THE CHRISTIAN BELIEF SYSTEM,
WHICH THE CHRISTIAN KNOWS TO BE GROUNDED IN
DIVINE REVELATION, IS RELEVANT TO ALL OF LIFE."
—*Carl F. H. Henry*[1]

GOD GLASSES

SEVENTH GRADE was not the best year to find out I needed glasses. As a young child, the thought of wearing glasses seemed cool. In fact, when

121

I was eight, I remember trying to fudge on an eye exam in order to convince the doctor I needed glasses. To my dismay, he found me found out, and I left the office that day without glasses.

In seventh grade, the way you look is a huge deal. That's the year you want to be without braces, pimples, and especially glasses. More than anything, you want to just blend in with everyone else.

Consequently, I remember hiding the fact that I was supposed to wear glasses. I would wear them in the car on the way to school, but take them off the moment I stepped foot into the hallways of my school.

Glasses are kind of funny. Without them, my whole perception of reality was jeopardized. Where I sat in class further complicated my vision problem. Of course, no one on the road to being cool sat in the front row. Thus, my friends and I officially claimed the back rows of Mr. Ryan's science class as "our territory." However, without my glasses, sitting in the back row made it extremely difficult to learn. I had to jot down blurry notes at best and trust that my friend's notes in their binder were the correct version of what came from Mr. Ryan's mouth.

More than once, on the days our tests were returned, because I chose not to wear my glasses, I found out that what I wrote on my paper was not what Mr. Ryan had written on the blackboard. My friends' notes were not the best help either because they were based on their interpretation of what Mr. Ryan said, not what he actually wrote down.

When I wore my glasses, my vision was sharp, clear, and crisp. I could perceive images, notes, and facial expressions. Without my glasses, my vision was blurry, compromised, and fuzzy. I couldn't identify words, concepts, or the world around me in an accurate manner. My glasses were the grid that accurately filtered the way I perceived the world around me. Regardless of how dumb I looked with them on, my glasses were essential if I wanted to see clearly.

Recently, I drove back from a youth conference in Virginia. More than 2,500 teens gathered for the sole purpose of worshiping God and His Word. God used the conference to convict me that lately I had not been wearing my God glasses. God glasses are the biblical worldview that shape and mold the way we perceive everything, including God, life, and culture. Without these God glasses, we're left up to our own faulty conclusions of how to interpret and interact with our world.

I was sitting in the conference wrestling with God. I thought to myself, "Gee, I'm really a good Christian. For heaven's sake, I'm a pastor. What do you mean I don't wear my God glasses? I read the Word all the time; it's my job."

The Holy Spirit spoke gently, cutting through layers of defensiveness. You may have God glasses, but you aren't wearing them. Just as you wore your glasses in the car and took them off when you stepped foot in the school, you're wearing your God glasses at church, but

> **GOD GLASSES ARE THE BIBLICAL WORLDVIEW THAT SHAPE AND MOLD THE WAY WE PERCEIVE EVERYTHING, INCLUDING GOD, LIFE, AND CULTURE.**

taking them off when you step foot in the world. You fail to wear them because you're trying to fit in with the world around you.

I reasoned, "What do you mean I don't wear them?"

A few months ago, in very subtle ways, I began taking off my God glasses. I was thinking about hell one day. You know, hell is a very offensive concept for a compassionate Christian. In fact, even Christian books are beginning to agree. A friend of mine introduced me to such a book the other day. It said, "Hell makes God a bloodthirsty monster who maintains an everlasting Auschwitz for His victims."[2]

The problem of intolerance is no easier. I recently spoke with a stranger in a camping store. "Christians are so narrow-minded," he said. He told me that all paths lead to God. In his mind, I was extremely arrogant for thinking that Jesus is the only way to heaven.

Without God glasses, other issues become fuzzy as well. Why does God allow pain and evil? Either He doesn't care, He can't do anything about it, or He is completely sadistic.

Where do babies go when they die? If all babies go to heaven, then (although I am completely against it) why doesn't the Christian community kill them all in order to ensure their eternal destiny? If all babies go to hell, God is without compassion and love.

Over the past few months, I had been removing my God glasses. In small subtle ways, when I came to a "test" day in my life, my first response was not, What would God think? but, What do I think? As a result, when the test results came back, just like with Mr. Ryan, I found out that what I believed was completely different than what God had written on His blackboard, the Bible.

In the journey on the road to relevance, it's so easy to remove our God glasses. We begin the conversation by asking man-centered questions. What movies can I watch? Should I only listen to Christian music? Should I separate myself from certain people, groups, or philosophies? Should I boycott businesses that promote pornography, homosexuality, or liberal agendas? How should I feel about the moral decay of society?

Some people fail to even ask any questions in reference to morality, media, and their role in faith and culture. These people justify their habits and behavior. A few of these rationalizations may be, "I don't care what people say; it's my life." "Scripture is so dry." "God is a God of love; He'll forgive my sin." "I can handle it, you don't see me going out and killing anyone or having an affair." "The Bible is cultural; it really does not apply to this situation." "We love each other; besides, marriage is just a piece of paper."

These questions and justifications are fundamentally the wrong place to start. They all begin with a man-centered view. Since they're the wrong questions, the wrong answers are invariably given. Before we begin talking about a proper view of the world and our role in it, we need to first talk about our need for glasses. A fundamental question in the conversation of relevance is not, "What do I think?" but rather, "What does God think?" This can only be answered when we're wearing our God glasses.

Job was a guy who took off his God glasses. In the book of Job, more than 330 questions are asked. Job asked God many questions concerning the problems of pain, evil, justice, and punishment. Job, although he started out wearing his God glasses, eventually he removed them, and his perception of life became blurry and fuzzy at best.[3]

God, in an attempt to reveal Job's need for God glasses, asks His own set of questions.[4] "Where were you when I laid the foundation of the earth? Have you ever in your life commanded the morning, and caused the dawn to know its place? Do you give the horse his might? Do you clothe his neck with a mane?"

Job gets the picture after God grills him with every type of question. Based on his reply, we can tell Job quickly put his God glasses back on.

Then Job replied to the Lord:

> *"I know that you can do all things; no plan of yours can be thwarted.*
> *Surely I spoke of things I did not understand, things too wonderful for me to know.*
> *You said, 'Listen now, and I will speak; I will question you, and you shall answer me.'*
> *My ears had heard of you but now my eyes have seen you. Therefore I despise myself and*
> *repent in dust and ashes."*
> *—Job 42:1-6*

When I fail to wear my God glasses, I'm left up to my own feelings and thoughts about faith, culture, and my role in both. Being a sinful man, that's a scary thought. With my glasses off, I can justify and rationalize habits, sins, and philosophies that are a direct offense to God and His Word. This shift is so subtle. At first, it's so innocent. However, the moment I start to filter life and culture through my own eyes is the moment I find myself on a path I don't care to be on.

Call it weak. Label me as a person who needs God as a crutch. Pronounce me dependent and naïve.

I'm glad the Department of Motor Vehicles restricts the visually impaired from driving a car. I'm a confident pedestrian knowing such people can't drive a car without glasses.

When people receive their driver's licenses, if they don't pass the vision test, they can't drive without wearing their glasses. Such people have a restriction printed on their license for everyone to know, especially the police. If such people drive without their glasses on, they're a threat to others, as well as themselves. Their cars become potential killing machines destroying anyone in their path.

So, as a Christian, why do I feel ashamed to admit I wear God glasses? The Bible already declares all people visually impaired.[5] God's solution for us, the spiritually visually impaired, is to wear God glasses.[6] So why do I resist from letting others know I need to wear them? Why do I struggle with admitting my handicap? I already know that when I drive my life without them on, I'm threatening to destroy my life or the lives of those who come into my path.

I thought a lot about life during the eight-hour trip home from the conference. In order to get my wife, the teens, and myself home safely, I wore my glasses as I drove the van back to Ohio. God spoke to my heart gently. In order to get to your real home safely, you'd better wear your God glasses.

"The lamp of your body is your eye; when your eye is healthy, your whole body also is full of light; but when it is bad, your body also is full of darkness."
—*Luke 11:34*

A BONE TO PICK

How can we combat the fact that most of us leave our faith at home or church when we head out in culture? What are some practical ways we can filter culture through our faith? If the key to integrating our faith with our culture is to have a God-centered view instead of a man-centered one, how does this happen? Simply, how do we put on our God glasses?

I think the major reason believers fail to integrate their faith with their culture is because they're experts in culture and novices in faith.

Most believers view theology as irrelevant, except for the professional minister. This is exactly what the Reformers fought against. They gave their life energies to return to a "priesthood of the believer" ideal, which put the Bible back into the hands of believers. Many modern day believers do the exact opposite. We willingly give our Bibles back to our ministers. We desire to return to a model that elevates clergy (pastors) and suppresses laity (non-pastors) as the ones who are experts in the Word.

For those who venture into Bible study or Sunday school, much of that learning is fragmented from other facets of life. The tendency is to isolate faith from real life. We do church on Sundays, but how that affects the way we live is unknown. As a result, our faith is only a small part of who we are, rather than a reservoir from which all of life flows.

Other people fail in that they mistake hearing for knowing. This too is a major thinking trap. In fact, people often train their senses to tune out information if they've heard it before, rationalizing that since they've heard it, they know it.

Hearing is centered upon the brief harnessing of information for temporary comprehension. Integration is centered upon long-term digestion for life-long application.

Hearing the Word is rooted in head knowledge. Integrating the Word is rooted in heart knowledge.

Many believers hear the Word of God, but never allow it to penetrate their hearts. Merely hearing the Word is motivated by external factors, such as impressing others, appearing spiritual, or increasing understanding. External motivation often leads to forgetfulness. Hearing is rooted in a short-term goal.

> **MANY BELIEVERS HEAR THE WORD OF GOD, BUT NEVER ALLOW IT TO PENETRATE THEIR HEARTS.**

Integrating the Word is motivated by an internal factor to learn. Internal motivation often leads to remembrance. It aims to learn for the purpose of application and proper use of knowledge. It has a long-term goal of transformation.

Our generation is an expert in culture. We have the latest scoop on everybody. We know the names of current movies, which are always changing, rather than the names of books in the Bible, which never change. Is just head knowledge the answer? Will knowing the sixty-six books of the Bible guarantee spirituality?

No way! However, spirituality can't happen without faith. Faith cannot happen without belief. Belief cannot happen without the knowledge of something. Let's face it, it's very difficult to believe something you don't know.[7]

Integrating our faith with our culture can only happen if we have a faith to integrate! When our faith is shallow, our hopes of transforming culture are shallow. In order for an agent to transform something, it has to be different from it. Many of us are no different than culture to begin with.

Notice, it was Paul who often quoted the "secular" poets. Think about Paul. He wasn't perfect. However, he had developed enough confidence in his faith to say to his hearers, "Follow me as I follow Christ."[8] Maybe you or I shouldn't begin to bother making our message relevant to our hearers until we first know the message ourselves! I would argue that until we can tell our hearers, follow me as I follow Christ, we're not ready to begin using "secular" things as a launching pad for biblical precedence. Paul wasn't in his formational stage of theological learning. He was well established and had dedicated himself to wholly understanding the Word.

Many people justify watching MTV 24/7 in order to minister to their peers. They reason that they have to know their culture to minister to their culture. Paul did observe the idols of his day, but his observation wasn't for pleasure or entertainment. In fact, while he observed the idols—which, by the way, was not a daily event he practiced—his spirit became provoked.[9] What he observed stirred him so much that he was motivated to preach the Gospel.[10]

Let's be honest though—the Bible is a pretty big book. How can we expect to integrate the Word when we can't even understand the Word? For most of us, the Bible is confusing, boring, and dead. Besides, if we were to start reading it with the purpose of integrating our faith with our culture, where we would we even start?

THE ELEMENTARY PRINCIPLES

I was never one of those kids in the smart math class. I guess I found all those rules and theorems a little too restrictive. I never ventured into pre-calculus. In fact, I barely made it through Algebra 2. I suppose my lack of knowledge in higher mathematics resulted from never getting a firm grasp on the basics. In those early days of education, my mind was more excited about play dough and recess. I wasn't grounded in the elementary principles, and so I could never build upon my shaky foundation.

In some ways, the spiritual world isn't much different than the world of mathematics. In fact, I see more similarities than I care to admit. Before nightmares of fractions and formulas come creeping back into your head, hear me out for a second.

The book of Hebrews reveals this reality. The author of Hebrews is less than excited about the condition of his readers. He talks about their foundation and their comprehension of the elementary principles, which are shaky at best.

> *For though by this time you ought to be teachers, you have need again for someone*
> *to teach you the elementary principles of the oracles of God,*
> *and you have come to need milk and not solid food. —Hebrews 5:12*

Did you catch it? The writer is saying that his readers don't have a firm grasp on the elementary principles of the Word. So, what's the result? They can't be teachers. They can't be transformists either. Instead, they have to relearn the basics and rebuild their foundation of the Word of God.

What are the timeless truths in this passage? I think there are two of them. If our generation fails to extract these two truths, then our hope of having a voice in culture will never come to fruition.

The first truth is that believers must have a firm grasp of the elementary principles themselves. Imagine a college math professor coming into a first grade class and teaching advanced calculus. We would find this scenario both repulsive and counterproductive. The professor would lose his audience in a moment because he can't relate advanced concepts to a class of kids that don't even grasp the basics. Yet, this is exactly what happens every day in the spiritual world.

In many of our churches, leaders are teaching on advanced levels of spirituality. They stand up on Sunday mornings and transfer complex biblical truth to congregations that are just as clueless as the first grade math class.

Is this the fault of the pastors and church leaders? No! We need more churches that don't dumb down the Scriptures, but preach the meat of the Word. However, we the learners need to do our homework and not sit around waiting for others to teach us the basics! The proof of knowing the basics is not regurgitating concepts onto paper once every six months. The proof of knowing the elementary principles is in the framework of practically applying the Word in our lives. If we reduce the basics to head knowledge, we'll just crank out a whole bunch of Pharisees.

Edward Farley, in *Theologia: The Unity and Fragmentation of Theological Education*, asked some simple yet profound questions:

> Why is it that the vast majority of Christian believers remain largely unexposed to Christian learning—to historical-critical studies of the Bible, to the content and structures of the great doctrines, to two thousand years of classic works on the Christian life, to the basic disciplines of theology, biblical languages, and Christian ethics? Why do bankers, lawyers, farmers, physicians, homemakers, scientists, salespeople, managers of all sorts, people who carry out all kinds of complicated tasks in their work and home, remain at a literalist, elementary school level in their religious understanding? How is it that high school age church members move easily and quickly into the complex world of computers, foreign languages, DNA, calculus, and cannot even make a beginning in historical-critical interpretation of a single text of Scripture? How is it possible one can attend or even teach in a Sunday school for decades and at the end of that time lack the interpretive skills of someone who has taken three or four weeks in an introductory course in the Bible at a university of seminary?

In addition, why are most of us ignorant concerning the elementary principles of the oracles of God, such as repentance from dead works, faith toward God, instruction about washings and laying on of hands, and the resurrection of the dead and eternal punishment?[11]

True, we're all at different places in our spiritual journeys. The problem is that some of us have been in that same place for ten or fifteen years. If someone asks me what God is doing in my life and I give them the same story about when I was five years old, then something is wrong. New Christians aren't supposed to know as much as seasoned saints. I've been humbled by the example of some new believers' appetites to consume the Word. Unfortunately, I think some of us veteran Christians fall into a rut where we're up on everyone else's latest view on spiritual issues, but not God's.

We need to spend less time giving our intellectual opinion on every cultural and societal issue that comes down the pipe. We need to know the message we're supposedly standing behind. Then we need to incarnate our theology into practical and thoughtful ways of loving our world. If we love people without knowing the elementary principles of God, then we're just a bunch of nice people.

The second truth we can extract from Hebrews 5 is that we need to communicate to the world on a level they can understand. We used to live in a "Christian" country. In years past, people grew up believing in The Ten Commandments, the Bible as the Word of God, and the facts about Noah's Ark. Today we're living in a biblically illiterate country. It doesn't know the basics. So when we share our faith with others, why do we start with advanced spiritual concepts?

> WE NEED TO SPEND LESS TIME GIVING OUR INTELLECTUAL OPINION ON EVERY CULTURAL AND SOCIETAL ISSUE THAT COMES DOWN THE PIPE.

Think about the way some present Jesus. "Let me tell you of God's love for you, His wonderful plan for your life, and His Son Jesus who died for you." How can people trust in someone they know nothing about? The best we can hope for from a biblically illiterate individual is a mixture of truth with error. When people mix their own views with the Gospel, this is what we call syncretism. Paul strictly warned against such a practice.[12]

When tribal missionaries go into a new field, to a people who have never heard the name of Christ, they start with the basics. We call this chronological teaching. They start with creation and teach through the Bible, all the way to Christ. They build a foundation with the elementary principles. Why? Because when the point of decision comes, they want people to believe in the Jesus the Bible presents, not a conglomeration of truth and error.

I believe if our generation ever hopes to fulfill the Great Commission— which is to make disciples, not converts—we better start with the elementary principles. We better get a firm grasp on the basics ourselves. Once we prove to know the basics by living them out in the context of real life with real people, then we can start teaching the basics to others.

Jesus, Philip, and Paul all taught advanced spirituality to their audiences.[13] In each one of these cases, their audiences had a deep knowledge of the basics. They came from backgrounds where they were exposed to the elementary principles. It was because of their foundation that they could receive deeper truth.

It would be sad to see a fifty-year-old in kindergarten sitting on a carpet square trying to tackle 3 + 4. Yet it seems like many seasoned saints cannot comprehend basic spiritual truths.

A wise friend of mine told me a brilliant statement: "We need to lower the bar on church, and raise the bar on discipleship."[14] I love this statement. We need to make Jesus "relevant" to the guy on the street. We need to become like children in order to see the kingdom of God. The woman at the well had a successful evangelistic campaign just by saying, "Come see a man who told me all the things I have done, this is not the Christ, is it?"[15]

However, we can't stop here. We need to press on to the meat of the Word. If the Bride of Christ is made up only of spiritual babies, we're in deep trouble. I believe our generation was made for so much more. I believe there's a growing interest among young adults to live out faith from a deep, centered theology. This theology isn't a sterile collection of doctrine. Rather, it's cutting edge, transformational truth that's integrated into every fiber of the individual.

GUIDING PRINCIPLES

Let's be honest—integrating our faith with our culture is difficult. We face much opposition on many different fronts. Ironically, often it's not these fronts that diffuse us. Instead, it's our own shallow faith. We need to be deeply rooted people with deeply rooted faith. We need to wear our God glasses everywhere we go.

Before wearing our God glasses, we first need to know what God glasses are! This happens as we begin to learn and practice the elementary principles. We never reach a place where we know and practice all of God's

Word. We're all on a journey. We're all attempting to integrate. None of us is all-knowing. So let's stop pretending we are.

The saint who is saved for only one day has something to learn and something to teach.[16] Likewise, the veteran believer who has been saved for a lifetime has something to learn and something to teach as well.[17]

Below are seven guiding principles for integrating faith into everyday life. These principles are both compelling and convicting. They remind me of the essential need for integration. I encourage you to chew on these seven principles. I believe if we really digest them, they'll help us dramatically in our journey towards a transformed mind. Remember, if we fail to integrate our faith with our culture, then we fail to be transformists.

Guiding Principles for Integrating Faith into Everyday Life

1. Theology is relevant and essential for everyone, regardless of his or her station in life.

2. Learning is an unending journey that one never graduates from.

3. Learning cannot be separated into the categories of "spiritual" and "secular."

4. Learning is incarnational and holistic (heart, soul, and mind) in nature.

5. The level of one's learning can only be measured in terms of how it has been practically applied in the life of the learner.

6. The learner should not have to justify the pursuit of wisdom in subjects dealing with God's second book (creation) because it harmonizes with God's first book (Scripture) since He is the Author of both.

7. Advanced learning, in any subject, cannot be pursued until the respective elementary principles have first been mastered.

BETTER THAN THE REAL THING

Do these principles sound too theoretical? Perhaps at this time in our journey, we should examine the life of someone in the twenty-first century. Maybe it's time to look at a real live person. I'm going to introduce you to one of my heroes. His story may be different than you'd expect. He's had his share of struggles, but the way he's handled them sets him apart. Regardless, in my eyes, he is the incarnation of a transformed mind.

Little children, let us not love with word or with tongue, but in deed and truth.
—1 John 3:18

MY JOURNAL IN THE JOURNEY

The Unknown
December 1999

Within lies that unique aspect that cries out
against conformity. Yet it's silenced. Yet
it's taught to remain voiceless in spite of
the need for something to be heard. Other
dimensions may describe their common
denominator as civilized tools that create
equality. Yet they never really stop to think
about the hell they created. Where all settle
for the lie that none are precious and all are
normal and of no value. Intellect fried and
creativity killed in the name of amusing
ourselves to death. And we settle for the lie
that's been sold with the sin it brings. Of
discipline and liberty of freedom and effort.
Remove the chains that hold you captive.
Free your mind from the fear of the unknown
roads and untraveled thoughts. Begin to fly
as you remove the flesh and familiarity of
pattern and routine and popular thought. Step
out. Reach within. Dare to dream. Start to live.
End the lie as you break the chains and encounter
the unknown.

CHAPTER 10=

THE INCARNATION OF A TRANSFORMED MIND

"HAVE YOU EVER WATCHED YOUR TWENTY-SIX-YEAR-OLD
WIFE SQUIRM IN COMPLETE AGONY, CALLING OUT TO GOD TO
TAKE AWAY HER PAIN, ONLY TO HAVE IT GROW WORSE?
I HAVE."

—*Palmer*

July 10, 2003 1:10 p.m.

I MET Mark Palmer back in 2001. My dad sat with him at a pastors'
retreat in Pennsylvania. He thought I might like to hang out with Palmer
since we were both ministering in the Columbus area. I called him, and we

chatted for a few minutes. He told me he'd love to meet, so we selected a local coffee shop as our place of introduction.

The moment I saw Palmer, I was a bit taken aback. Any guy that stands over 6'8" has that effect on people I suppose. We ordered a drink and told our stories.

We talked about philosophy, music, our wives, and mostly about Jesus— only, the way he talked about Jesus was a little bit strange. It was as if the Jesus Palmer talked about was real. I mean, of course I know Jesus is real, but the stories Palmer shared made it seem like he'd literally spent the day before hanging out with the incarnated Son of God.

I sat there with a barrage of emotions. I felt intrigued, curious, nervous, perplexed, and mostly excited. This guy had a strange quality about him. He seemed relevant. Isn't that what we all want?

Palmer came across without any separatist tendencies. I sat back waiting for the conformist tendencies to come spilling out ... only they didn't.

I began to probe and pick at his theology, searching for a crack in his worldview. Once again, I couldn't find any. Philosophically, we agreed on many things, but his methodology seemed so foreign to me. As he explained the way he did church, I thought I was hearing a rendition of the early Church from the book of Acts. Nonetheless, after a while, I was convinced his theology was sound.

Following our time at the coffee shop, he drove me around the neighborhood. He had a house church, which he referred to as a missional community. Both its name and location were definitely nontraditional. The community, called The Landing Place, took up roots in a section just north of downtown Columbus called the Short North.[1] Many of the buildings we passed had large murals painted on them. As we drove through the streets, it was obvious that this part of town was splashed with a progressive artistic feel.

As I left that day and headed home, Palmer handed me a business card. On it was a little alien in a spaceship. The card read The Landing Place. I looked for his job title. Instead of it saying "Pastor" or "Church Planter," his self-made title read: "Mark Palmer: Resident Instigator." I liked Mark, and so began our friendship.

MORE ABOUT PALMER

A few months later, I called up Mark to come talk to the young adult group at my church. We wanted our wives to meet, so we grabbed some dinner before the gathering that night. Mark, Jennifer, Kelly, and I hit it off. We shared our experiences in the ministry and talked about our college lives. We each took turns telling the story of how we met, fell in love, and got married. Mark and Jennifer told us they were expecting a child in a few months.

Eventually, we headed over to the young adult gathering. Palmer had a Q & A time about ministry in the Short North. Every time I hung out with him, my theology was forced out of the box and into real life. I found myself subconsciously saying inside, "That's not the way it's supposed to be done." However, when I examined the Scriptures, he was consistent.

> THE STORIES PALMER SHARED MADE IT SEEM LIKE HE'D LITERALLY SPENT THE DAY BEFORE HANGING OUT WITH THE INCARNATED SON OF GOD.

I asked Palmer to tell me a little more about The Landing Place and his philosophy of ministry. He gave me the facts:

The Landing Place is a community of friends and neighbors that "do life" together. The central theme of this life is a shared passion for following Jesus. We often gather in each others' homes to share meals, have conversations, read Scriptures, tell stories, study the teachings of Jesus, sing songs, pray prayers, recite poetry, and practice liturgies.

Sometimes a few of us will meet in a coffeehouse or pub for spiritual and/or philosophical discussion, or to talk about a book we've currently read and found meaningful.

We also like to throw worship parties in our art studio. Our parties usually involve some or all of the following: candles, loud music, incense, quiet music, visual art, food, sitting, standing, meditation, dialogue, monologue, songs, and ancient prayers.

There are certain things we value that shape who we are as a church. They are:

Following Jesus (because we consider Him to be not only the finest teacher who ever lived, but also the Messiah).

Being Creative (because we are made in the image of the Creator, and seek to make Him known through our creations).

Sharing Life (because life is best experienced together in community).

Making Peace (because Jesus asked us to not only love our friends, but also our enemies).

Loving Our Neighbors (because being a good neighbor is one of the most valuable things you can do).

The Story (because to value the lives of those who have gone before us is to make our own stories richer).

Living Missionally (because living as a "sent" people allows people to see Jesus, and experience Him for themselves).

We are artists, students, thinkers, parents; but more than anything, we're just people on a journey. We always enjoy meeting new friends who are also on the journey. Hopefully we can meet soon over a cup of coffee and a story.

Like I thought—simple, inspiring, and incarnational. I was gripped by Mark and Jennifer's commitment to faith and culture. Certainly this was a couple that didn't reject the culture in which they lived. Surprisingly, they didn't conform to their culture either. They transformed it!

The culture they lived within was certainly unique. Everyone native to the Columbus area knows that the Short North certainly has the characteristic of being unique. One source describes this part of town as a stretch "containing a variety of places to eat and shop mixed in with dozens of art galleries. The Short North is also a popular nightlife destination with dozens of bars and clubs lining high street."[2]

Another source contextualized this section of the city as, "Columbus' version of New York's artsy Soho district, this historic urban neighborhood is filled with boutiques, art galleries, coffee houses, restaurants and theaters."[3] These generous words could not always be attributed to this area.

In fact, less than twenty years ago, it "was known for dilapidated buildings, crime, drugs, and prostitution. The name 'Short North' was used by police to describe the run down area between downtown Columbus and the Ohio State University."[4]

Anyway you slice it, the Short North is a place, just like any other place in this world, that is in desperate need of Christ. The Palmers knew this and therefore committed their lives to bringing light to this corner of darkness. The amazing thing is that they balanced their faith with the culture of the Short North in some pretty transformational ways.

I loved what I saw and wanted a piece of it. I took a group of teens downtown to pitch in and give Palmer a hand. We painted, cleaned, swept, and organized something he called the Kindergarten room. That afternoon we set up shop on his front porch and cooked hot dogs for neighbors and strangers passing by. It was just a simple way we loved God and people.

Palmer sent me more stuff about some upcoming events at The Landing Place. Once again, I was intrigued at the simplicity. Once again, I saw a couple that was consciously living as transformists. Here were just some of their events.

The Kindergarten Room

The Kindergarten Room was an all-ages music and art space we did last year. We hosted visual artists, poetry readings, and live music. This was basically an effort to create an atmosphere where people could meet people and to allow artists a venue to express themselves in meaningful ways. It was an opportunity for people to tell their stories in ways that were important to them. We hosted local visual artists in a gallery setting; my housemate Aaron hosted a poetry reading series called The Switchboard Series, and we hosted local and national bands in the space. It was pretty great all around.

Worship Parties

The Eucharist (bread and cup) is always the focal point. Musicians write music. Worshipers write lyrics. Poets write poems. Painters paint. All these forms of worship are impromptu. It's a really nice vibe.

Labyrinth

All the cool kids are doing it. Individuals walk through a prayer path guided by a CD.

Small White Light

The Landing Place community takes things like Advent, Epiphany, Lent, and Pentecost pretty seriously. Last year for Advent, we did original music and readings from our community. These all focused on the past and future comings of Jesus.

Catacomb Worship

Gathered in self-created catacombs to celebrate the lives of saints who have gone before us—Bonhoeffer, Nouwen, St. Francis, etc. Our community celebrated their lives through their transformational writings. In a setting of candles, we sang songs and celebrated the Eucharist.

Urban Monastic Communities

More and more of us are moving toward sharing our lives on more intimate levels. For some of us, that means actually living together, sharing the same space and possessions.

Book Groups

In local coffeehouses. We do this by just sitting down and being present (that's most of what mission is). We invite others to dialogue around a book and go on a journey with us. We've done *Sex, Economy, Freedom, and Community* by Wendell Berry and *My Confession, My Religion* by Leo Tolstoy.

Being Good Neighbors

I mean, love your neighbor as yourself, right? This might take the form of mowing their lawns, being with their kids, or having cookouts ... so simple.

THE TWO BECAME ONE

Why do I write about Mark? What's so significant about him? As I cautioned in chapter two, there is a danger in reading a book about how to balance faith and culture. The danger is that we read it and fail to live it. It's an easy thing to write a book about how to balance faith and culture; it is a whole different matter to live a life that balances faith and culture. Mark and Jennifer have done such a thing.

I wanted you to see the incarnation of a transformist in someone other than Jesus or Paul. I wanted you to see the practical things they do to transform culture, without becoming compromised by it.

Without incarnation, we are just theorists. Without our paradigm infused into the life of a real person with a set of real issues, we're only speculating. What makes us relevant is incarnation.

> IT'S OUT OF AN INTENSE AND AUTHENTIC STRUGGLE THAT MARK IS ABLE TO TRANSFORM THE CULTURE AROUND HIM.

Mark had no idea the real set of issues he, Jennifer, and their baby Micah were about to face. Only the Father knew the events that would befall these transformists. The two would become one.

Transformists don't just transform culture when everything is going well. They aren't exempt from intense trial and pain. They aren't fickle people who only love God when it's easy. They struggle because faith is a struggle.

As I've observed Mark's life, I've seen he's exactly this type of person. He doesn't love God with lip service or surface obedience. Rather, it's out of an intense and authentic struggle that Mark is able to transform the culture around him. Other than sharing Palmer's own heart with you, I don't know a better way to explain the significant events surrounding the summer of 2003. Below are his journal entries that record some of his darkest and brightest moments.

Date: 2003-07-04 13:14

Wanted to pass along an update on our journey. Jennifer finished her second round of chemotherapy a few weeks ago, and on Monday had the first CT scans since beginning treatment. We received the results of those scans on Wednesday. The scans showed that the cancer has doubled in size, and has spread further in a very aggressive way. Because of this, Jennifer will not be continuing her current form of treatment. The doctor also did not want her to continue eating any longer, because of the damage it could cause to her digestive system. So yesterday, Jennifer was admitted to the hospital to begin receiving TPN, which is nutrition that is fed through the central line in her chest. After this weekend, she will be able to receive that at home, at night, while she is sleeping. The TPN will provide her body with all of the nutrition that it needs. We now need to decide together what direction we will take concerning further treatment of the cancer.

The news we received was obviously disappointing. But Jennifer and I continually reminded each other in the days leading up to the test that no matter what the results were, it didn't change who God was, or what He wanted to do for her. God still is who He is. His will is still for Jennifer to be completely whole and healthy and disease free (that is His will for all of His children). It doesn't change the fact that the death and resurrection of Jesus of Nazareth 2,000 years ago provided for not only our spiritual healing, but for our physical as well. It doesn't change the fact that the kingdom has come among us in the person of that same Jesus, although not yet in its fullness ...

And so it doesn't change what our responsibility is: to lay hands on the sick, and to pray that they will be healed, and to believe that God desires that same thing very much. And do please continue to pray for Jennifer's healing, joining us in believing that her good Father desires it even more than we do.

Be encouraged. Don't lose heart. The battle is not over. Our family blesses you as you fight this battle with us. "Father in Heaven, holy is Your name. Your kingdom come, Your will be done, here on earth, just as it is in heaven."

Date: 2003-07-09 13:10

Have you ever watched your twenty-six-year-old wife squirm in complete agony, calling out to God to take away her pain, only to have it grow worse?

I have.

(When will Your healing come?)

After Mark wrote this entry, two anonymous readers took a risk and replied. This is just a glimpse of the Body of Christ at work. Evidently, none of us are immune to pain.

Date: 2003-07-09 (Anonymous)

I lost my husband when he was thirty-six years old, after spending five years in the process of dying. He was a juvenile diabetic, and complications had set in.

I never felt so forgotten by God in my life. I was completely on my own.

He lost limbs and suffered from phantom pain; he was on peritoneal dialysis and suffered from the pain of having his gut stretched with fluid. He had neuropathy pain. He never got better. And it went on, and on, and on.

These things happen, have to happen. And I don't blame God for it or demand His mercy in them. But it's just not fair. And yes, I am still angry about it.

But it is. The reality is in front of you. Don't hesitate to use whatever means you must to try to make her comfortable—it's all you can do.

And pray. I always felt better.

Date: 2003-07-09 18:37 (Anonymous)

Oh honey, I am so sorry for your pain. I do not know why I keep reading your journal. I do not even know you, and yet I keep finding myself here. Maybe I can relate in one way. I have a fifteen-month-old daughter, and I can only imagine the pain of having to leave her. It is so amazing to me that you can keep praying and keep your faith. She must be so sad to leave her son; it totally breaks my heart. I cry almost every night thinking about the three of you. I will continue to pray for you and her healing. He is all-powerful, and can heal in His time. Take care—God bless you all.

Date: 2003-07-10 10:42

Long night ... we had to take Jennifer to the emergency room around midnight last night; we just couldn't get the pain under control with the morphine. Surprisingly, it was our first trip to emergency since Jennifer's diagnosis. Hopefully our last trip as well. Around 5 a.m., they finally decided to check her in. She's on some pretty heavy pain medicine right now, so is feeling better.

Interesting the timing of it all. Last night, around 8 or 9, my housemate Aaron and friend Brandon spent some time praying for me. The Spirit of God was really present in a strong way, strengthening me and encouraging me. It was right on time.

Pretty tired right now. I think I'll go take a nap with my son.

Date: 2003-07-30 21:31

I thought I would post an update on Jennifer and the journey that we have been on for a few months now. We were in Cincy two weekends ago, worshiping and sharing life with friends from around the region. Jennifer had a really wonderful time; she was strong and was encouraged by all the prayers and love we received while there. When we returned on Monday, she became very tired, and then started to experience nausea on Thursday. The nausea became so severe on Sunday that I took her to the emergency room, and we spent the night in the hospital.

While there, she began to have waste drain from the tube in her stomach. Her doctor told me this indicated the stomach and the bowels had fused and that waste was passing freely into her abdomen. This was what was causing the nausea. He encouraged us to bring her home, so that she could be comfortable for her last days here on earth. While at the hospital, we also made the most difficult decision I have ever been faced with, to stop her nutrition. It was only feeding the tumors and making her more sick. So as of Saturday evening, Jennifer is no longer receiving any nutrition for her body to live.

We came home Monday evening, and have been controlling the nausea with around the clock injections of medicine. Jennifer is sometimes aware, and sometimes not. This morning we spent a few hours together in the gardens behind the house, talking of the future, the past, and how unimaginably wonderful it will be when she meets God.

I also told her that I still believed God could heal her, and renewed my promise to pray for that until the end. I would encourage you to join me in that prayer, asking God to bring His healing in a miraculous way. I know that if Jennifer had the strength to write, she would say the same thing.

She would also say to be encouraged. Do not lose heart. The kingdom is present.

Date: 2003-08-01 11:48

Last night 64 King was filled with the laughter and conversation and tears of our spiritual community. We shared a meal, as we always do, and then began to sing songs to our God. Jennifer was not able to come down, because she was too weak. So we all gathered in the entryway, up the stairway, and down the hall that leads to our bedroom. There we continued to sing, and Jennifer joined us ...

> **THE SPIRIT OF GOD WAS REALLY PRESENT IN A STRONG WAY, STRENGTHENING ME AND ENCOURAGING ME. IT WAS RIGHT ON TIME.**

Rejoice, lift up your voice and praise Jesus now
Hallelujah

Our Father in heaven holy is Your name
Your kingdom come, Your will be done here

When we were done, I whispered to Jennifer that what she had just experienced was but a tiny taste of kingdom come.

She smiled.

Date: 2003-08-09 18:35

I want to again say thank you to all of you for your prayers and encouragement during this journey. They have really sustained us during this unimaginably difficult time. God is so gracious to us. The last few days have been filled with questions for me, questions of why God might be sustaining Jennifer this long. Thursday night she was able to come downstairs and worship with our community of faith. It was really amazing; she had been pretty unresponsive most of the day, but as we began to sing, she mouthed the words along with us, basking in the beauty of community and worship ...

Date: 2003-08-12 09:23

Friends,

This morning at 6 a.m., Jennifer's spirit went to be with her Father God. Her physical body awaits the resurrection of the dead on the day of the Lord. We live this life to the glory of God. We anxiously wait for the next life to begin. All praise to Jesus of Nazareth, the Resurrected One.

The funeral was a solemn celebration. People from their community of faith testified one after the other about Jennifer and Mark's life of faith. There were courageous stories. Some were joyful. And others were wrapped with sorrow.

So what? Is Mark Palmer removed from the pain? Is it easy to raise Micah alone? Because he is a follower of Jesus, does that mean everything is okay?

Date: 2003-08-12 22:13

It's 10 p.m., and I am frightened of going upstairs to bed by myself. I have gone to sleep with Jennifer every night for the last five-plus years, and now I am quite unsure of how to do it myself.

If you are awake this evening, will you pray with me through the watches of the night?

Thirty-eight people posted a message to Mark this night. That evening, although Jennifer was not physically there, Mark did not go to bed exclusively by himself.

Date: 2003-08-21 13:51

It's the little things that trigger memory, and the grief that waits patiently in the background until it is stirred … receiving junk mail addressed to Jennifer, finding pieces of her hair in random places around the house, getting in the car and hearing the CD that was playing on our last trip to the hospital over three weeks ago that I have yet to remove from the player, deciding to finally open the mail at 1 a.m. and having Jennifer's death certificate be the first thing I open … with all my strength I tried to put it down; I ended up reading it word for word. Twice.

> SEEING MARK IN THESE MONTHS OF PAIN, SORROW, AND REJOICING HAS MADE THE INCARNATION ALL THE MORE REAL.

It all adds up to a longing and a loneliness the nature of which cannot be described in words.

Date: 2003-09-09 13:58

The nice cashier at Lowe's gave Micah a flower this morning "to take home to his mommy." It's stuff like that, which just comes out of nowhere and blindsides you.

THE REAL INCARNATION

Seeing Mark in these months of pain, sorrow, and rejoicing has made the incarnation all the more real. I have no answers for why God took Jennifer and left Mark and his one-year-old son Micah alone. None of us has a complete perspective.

Palmer has maintained his steady course of being a transformist. This has only been possible through his commitment to God and the commitment of God's people to him. The next few months and years will be a grieving process. He seems stronger in some ways, and weaker in others. Nonetheless, he is a transformist. He has balanced loving God and people with his faith and culture. He is the incarnation of a transformed mind, and I thank him for his inspiring example to me.

But we do not want you to be uninformed, brethren, about those who are asleep, that you may not grieve, as do the rest who have no hope. For if we believe that Jesus died and rose again, even so God will bring with Him those who have fallen asleep in Jesus. Therefore comfort one another with these words.

—1 Thessalonians 4:13-14, 18

MY JOURNAL IN THE JOURNEY

Breathe
December 1999

Your smile melts so much resistance. Your
soul chips away the walls of ugliness, the
years of faded paint that once glistened in
the sunlight of my dreams. Those are spent
and shot. Crackled and crumbling. Broken
and stumbling. Bruised and beaten. Twisted
and torn. Fatigued and worn. Those darts sank
deep into my flesh, the humanity screaming in
its curdling manner, in its commonness that
plagues this placid landscape, emerging and
converging and containing and maintaining the
essence of me. Now I rise, I stand, I am once again
renewed. Too ignorant to cease dreaming.
Too foolish to refrain from believing. I am
empowered, enthralled, inspired, and encouraged
To begin to die. To end all beginnings. To silence
all absence of noise. To live. For within that
moment I took the steps of freedom. Looking at you,
I seized the instrument of liberty, placed it against my
head, pulled the trigger, and began to breathe.

CHAPTER 11=

A GLOBAL MOVEMENT

"WE MUST GET BEYOND TEXTBOOKS, GO OUT INTO THE
BY-PATHS AND UNTRODDEN DEPTHS OF THE WILDERNESS
AND TRAVEL AND EXPLORE AND TELL THE WORLD THE
GLORIES OF OUR JOURNEY."

—*John Hope Franklin*

IN SOME respects, our journey is nearing an end. In another sense, it's
only beginning. We've wandered down the road to relevance, encountering
the Divine and the depraved. We've stared straight into the eyes of the
irrelevant extremes within us all. We've heard inspiring tales of transformists

153

who have gone before. So what's next? What now?

Good question. The difference between a nice book and a movement is the people who read it. You're the difference.

Disagree with the book. Dissect the book. But please don't dismiss the book and label it as ... well, nice. I think any member of the current generation owes it to himself or herself and the watching world to seriously interact with this age-old/cutting edge dilemma. Too much is at stake, like eternity for instance.

You have a choice. The real power is not in a book. It may ignite a movement, but it only brings the conversation to the table. Critics can accept or reject it. The real influence is in the incarnated life of a transformist. No one can argue with a relevant life. No one can dismiss someone who balances loving God and people with their faith and culture.

Call me a dreamer. Call me a fool. I believe only you can decide where we must go next. I believe you need to start a global movement within your sphere of influence.

HOW DO I START A GLOBAL MOVEMENT?

First you need to ask yourself if you really believe the life of a transformist can be incarnated. If you don't believe it, then set this book on the shelf and flip on the TV. If you do believe the life of a transformist can be incarnated, then you need to understand four fundamental truths.

The status of a transformist is only maintained; it's never attained this side of heaven.
You may lose something.
You will gain something.
You will fail.

Let's unwrap these, one at a time.

The status of a transformist is only maintained; it's never attained this side of heaven.

Solomon, the wisest man who ever lived, failed to grasp this, and it led him to his ruin. He made the grave mistake of thinking his wisdom was attained instead of maintained. Do you remember the story?

> *The LORD appeared to Solomon in a dream at night;*
> *and God said, "Ask what you wish me to give you."*
> —*1 Kings 3:5*

As already mentioned, Solomon asked God to give him "an understanding heart to judge Thy people to discern between good and evil."[1] The content of his request is a major clue that he was already in a close relationship with God. God was so thrilled at Solomon's request that He gave him a heart full of wisdom more than anyone who ever

THE WISEST MAN WHO EVER LIVED CAME TO RUIN FOR ONE SINGLE REASON. SOLOMON DEPARTED FROM A CLOSE RELATIONSHIP WITH THE LORD.

lived before or after. In addition, God gave Him riches and honor.

End of story, right? Unfortunately, the wisest man who ever lived came to ruin for one single reason. Solomon departed from a close relationship with the Lord. He didn't heed the Lord's words to his father David, "If your sons are careful of their way, to walk before Me in truth with all their heart and with all their soul, you shall not lack a man on the throne of Israel."[2]

Instead, this wise and discerning man, a transformist to the core, lost everything because he failed to maintain his relationship with God. As a result, the Lord said to Solomon, "Because you have done this, and you have not kept My covenant and My statutes, which I have commanded you, I will surely tear the kingdom from you, and will give it to your servant."[3]

Solomon failed to see that wisdom is not an inherent part of humanity. It's not a separate entity from God, but it's found in and through a relationship with Him.

The status of a transformist must be maintained. The moment we think it's attained and move from maintaining a relationship with God, we fail to be transformists.

You may lose something.

There are tales of transformists everywhere you look. Movies are filled with them. In fact, they're the ones that grip our hearts the most. *Braveheart, Anne of Green Gables, Gladiator,* and *Les Miserables* are all centered around the life of a transformist. The truth is that each of these transformists lost something along the way.

Some lost their lives. Others lost control. Still others lost their jobs, status, friends, family, or the former way of doing things. Most of us want to be like these relevant people. But like them, are we willing to lose something?

Ironically, each of these movies has supporting characters that are separatists and/or conformists. Strangely, they're all cast in an irrelevant light. Some follow the path the transformist cut. Others fail to move from their irrelevant extreme. Regardless, if they allowed themselves to be transformed, they too had to lose something. Some lost fear. Others lost concern. Still others lost apathy, grudges, rules, or safety.

Are you willing to lose something? It's easy to desire the life of a transformist. It's difficult to actually live one.

I met a former pastor at a wedding. He told me how he lost his job. He was nothing more than a transformist, and it cost him his financial security, his standing in the community, and his promise of a career.

I know a young couple that packed up all their belongings and headed to Papua New Guinea. Their only goal is to share the love of Christ with the tribe they live in. When they need to receive a routine medical procedure, they fly out of the country all the way to Australia. They and their two little ones have willingly chosen to lose a comfortable life for the sake of others.

I know a young lady who is now alone because she will not give in to pressure. She has chosen not to settle for less than God's best for her. As a result, on Friday and Saturday nights, she is without a man. She lost any hope of getting married soon.

If you're going to live the life of a transformist, be ready to lose something. Inevitably, it will always happen. Most often, you'll lose something you never planned on.

You will gain something.

Without a doubt, you'll gain something in return. This too is often unplanned. It's just like God to surprise us.

I know a man who gained purpose as he lost his fear. I know a couple that gained their relationship back as they lost their pride. I knew a woman who gained peace as she lost her life.

God wants to give us something better. It's not always what we want or what we think we need. The life of a transformist is one of giving up, but in a strange twist, it's one of getting back.

"For whoever wishes to save his life shall lose it,
but whoever loses his life for My sake, he is the one who will save it." —*Luke 9:24*

You will fail.

You might as well get it through your head that you're going to fail. The life of a transformist is one of failing. If this is true, why try? The alternative is no alternative at all. The life of a separatist or conformist is one of a failure! There is no risk. Thus, these irrelevant people have failed before they've even tried.

Logic says that safety breeds success. Both the separatist and conformist sleep in safety. Neither extreme dares to struggle. One retreats from everything, while the other accepts everything. Both fail to transform anything.

In the gym, the guy who never lifts any weight never fails. He simply is just a failure. The guy who dares to put up weight—even if he fails, he succeeds. He breaks down his muscle in order to build it up again. He'll see and experience results because he dares to fail.

Transformists will fail. The key is not how or when you fail, but if you get up again. Growth only happens in the presence of adversity. It's our faith that pleases God.[5] He wants us to take Him at His Word.

When I lived the life of a separatist or conformist, my record was undefeated. Strangely though, those were the days I felt the most defeated.

Just like in most aspects of following Jesus, spiritual healthiness is a paradox. When we're weak, we're strong. When we fail, we succeed.

If we've any hope of creating a global movement of transformists, we must get this through our heads. We must extend grace to fellow transformists. There is a risk, but not only is it worthwhile, it's necessary.

When people venture out beyond their safe irrelevant extremes, you need to encourage them. They, like you and I, will fail. Nonetheless, they're living the life of faith. You know what will kill a transformist? It will be a brother or sister kicking them when they're down.

One of the major factors that helped me break out of my irrelevant extremes was the great group of people God put around me. Kelly was a major player in that, so I married her. I should say, she married me! I had mentors, counselors, and friends pushing for me.

One time I failed big time. I took a huge fall. Sadly, a brother and sister kicked me real hard when I was already down. I take it back. They didn't kick me; they took their feet and grounded my face into the asphalt. Afterwards, I fled back to irrelevance and almost remained for good. I knew it was safer.

Being a separatist or conformist is safer! Ironically, I learned that the place where safety is probably is the place where faith isn't.

God convinced me I needed to get back up and try again. Now I never want to go back to irrelevance. The life of a transformist is the only life I want.

Will I fail again? You bet! Will I fall on the ground again? Will a so-called brother or sister hold me down? Yes! Yes! Will I remain in an irrelevant extreme? I hope not!

Let us labor therefore to enter into that rest,
lest any man fall after the same example of unbelief. —Hebrews 4:11

BE A STUDENT

Not everyone needs to "do church" like Mark Palmer. Please understand me, it's not the external things Mark has done that make him relevant. The reason why Palmer has struck such a chord in my own life is that his relevancy is internal. Mark, out of his love for God, will not compromise the non-negotiables. His life and his ministry are all about Jesus.

Some people may react to the way Palmer does relationship with God and people. They may miss the whole point and think Mark's methodology is what sets him apart. They may reduce his community of faith to a group of people who tell stories and light incense.

Jesus, Paul, and Mark Palmer all did something similar. They were students of the culture in which they found themselves. Jesus loved God and people. He studied the culture that surrounded Him. Likewise, Paul (as seen in Acts 17) studied his culture.

Interestingly, Paul adapted his methodology of ministry to the specific needs of the culture in which he found himself.

Palmer has adapted his methodology to the culture within the Short North. If Mark went to Africa or Europe, I bet his faith would still be relevant. Why? Regardless of the geography in which we find ourselves, one language is universal. One voice speaks beyond cultural, societal, and racial boundaries. This is the language of love. Loving God and loving people is the essence of relevance.

What culture do you find yourself in? Where is your place in life? Are you a college student, a nurse, a factory worker, a husband? Are you a father, a sister, a homemaker? Are you in America, Australia, an island in the South Pacific?

In order to be a transformist, you may need to adapt some external things in order to reach the people around you. You may need to dress a little different or "do church" a little different. All these things are secondary though. You will be relevant if above all else, you love God and people.

REDEEM THE DAY

Transformists realize the power of the present.

Redeeming the time, because the days are evil. —Ephesians 5:16 (KJV)

Time is a mystery. It's a sacred trust. It's something we're all given and something we all spend. Time is subjective and elusive. It's fleeting. Our lives are set by it. We believe we control time, but for most of us, it ends up controlling us. Time is temporal, and yet it has eternal impact.

To "seize" means to take hold of. Most people long to make their lives extraordinary and intend to do so by seizing the day. Seizing deals with spending time.

To "redeem" means to buy back. The few people who actually make their lives extraordinary do so by redeeming the day. Redeeming deals with investing time.

The Greek word *exagorazo* (ex-ag-or-ad'-zo), translated in the English "redeem," literally means "to buy back." Transformists seek to buy back time by investing, impacting, and influencing others. They perpetuate a lifestyle of no regret because they take advantage of the here and now. They transform the future by redeeming the present.

Much of today's generation is killing time. Most of our lives are filled with intentional distraction. This killing of time is wounding eternity.

So how do you buy back time?

One can only buy back time by investing in eternal things. Only two things in this life are eternal: people, and simple acts of love done in Jesus' strength for Jesus' name.

Life is fast. Time is short. Redeem the day.

So teach us to number our days, That we may present to Thee a heart of wisdom.
—*Psalm 90:12*

WITHIN YOUR SPHERE OF INFLUENCE

The world is a big place, and you are a small person. A huge concept is for you to actually transform culture. Where do you start?

"Transform" means to "change the character or nature of."[4]

"Culture" is the "beliefs, behaviors, customs, and institutions of a given group of people at a given point in time."[5]

So how do you change the character or nature of the beliefs, behaviors, customs, and institutions of a given group of people at a given point in time?

Try this on for starters:

Love God and people. Balance faith and culture. Tell the message.

Be patient with separatists and conformists. God is dealing with them. But share your story. Most people know there is an alternative out there. They just don't know what it is.

Believe you have influence. Each one of us has someone in our lives willing to listen. Take a risk. Step out. Speak up. Pull a chair up to the conversation. Who cares if you don't have all the answers? You know who does. Point people to Him.

Get off the fence. Get off the shelf. Get off the bench.

Get in the game. Get in the adventure. Get in the journey.

Stay on the road. Stay off the ground. Stay hungry.

Don't look down. Don't look around.

Don't give up. Don't give in. Don't give out.

Keep walking. Keep talking.

Don't shut up. Don't shut down. Don't sell out.

No reserve. No retreat. No regret.

Invest. Impact. Influence others.

Share. Speak. Shout.

Tell tales of transformation. Draft writings on relevance. Flesh out ideas for incarnation.

Redeem the day!

PARTING WORDS

The road to relevance is a long journey. It's an exciting journey. It's the only journey. I pray you have found both conviction and courage to continue the journey.

Remember, as transformists ...

We don't need to have everything figured out, for that would mean we're separatists. We don't need to say anything goes, for that would mean we're conformists.

We're not perfect, for none of us are. However, we're seekers. We long to have a simple and unadulterated relationship with the Creator of the universe. We desire to know the "why" behind the "what" and the purpose behind the principle. Of course, there will be mistakes along the way, but this is what sets us believers apart. We have a little more grace and patience with each other, because we know what we've been saved from.

The movement is beginning. The gathering has united. We come from a variety of backgrounds, but share a common purpose. Above all else, we passionately love God and people in proper balance. We're not afraid of culture because our mission transcends it. We're not afraid of religion because our method surpasses it. We are the relevant. We are the transformists.

"And it will come about in all the land," Declares the LORD,
"That two parts in it will be cut off and perish; But the third will be left in it.
And I will bring the third part through the fire, Refine them as silver is refined, And test
them as gold is tested. They will call on My name, And I will answer them; I will say,
'They are My people,' And they will say, 'The LORD is my God.'"
—Zechariah 13:8-9

YOUR JOURNAL IN THE JOURNEY

THE NEXT CHAPTER

"I FEEL AS IF I AM WALKING WITH DESTINY,
AND THAT ALL MY PAST LIFE HAS BEEN BUT A PREPARATION
FOR THIS HOUR AND FOR THIS TRIAL."
—*Winston Churchill*

The next chapter is yours to write.
What will it say?

Please share your story.
www.redeemtheday.org

INDEX OF FIGURES

ENDNOTES

PREFACE
1. John 5:3
2. Ephesians 5:22-32; Revelation 19:7; 21:2
3. Matthew 5:13-16

CHAPTER I
1. Most every illustration breaks down on some level. The purpose of comparing the Garden of Eden scenario with our modern day dilemma is to expose the reality that separatists and conformists have existed since the beginning. These camps have not just arrived on the scene. I believe that Adam and Eve were sinless until they ate the fruit, thus disobeying God. However, even in the manner they faced temptation, we can see unique tendencies. These tendencies (those of the separatist and those of the conformist) are not sinful in and of themselves, but the outcome of these tendencies, if not held in check, can soon conceive sin.
2. Genesis 1:28-29
3. Genesis 2:16-17
4. Genesis 3:11, 17
5. Emphasis mine
6. John 17:14-18
7. God has not left us without a clue (2 Timothy 3:16-17), but many of us choose to live that way.

CHAPTER 2
1. Merriam-Webster, *Merriam-Webster's Collegiate Dictionary, 11th Edition* (Merriam-Webster, Inc: July 2003).
2. James 2:14-26
3. Luke 10:30-37

CHAPTER 3
1. "'And the Word became flesh' (John 1:14), he says. The terms he employs here are not terms of substance, but of personality. The meaning is not that the substance of God was transmuted into that substance which we call 'flesh.' 'The Word' is a personal name of the eternal God; 'flesh' is an appropriate designation of humanity in its entirety, with the implications of dependence and weakness. The meaning, then, is simply that He who had just been described as the eternal God became, by a voluntary act in time, a man." Geoffrey W. Bromiley, *The International Standard Bible Encyclopedia Vol. 1-4* (Grand Rapids: William B. Erdmans Publishing Company, 1979).
2. John 1:14
3. Many applaud Morpheus for exhorting Neo in *The Matrix* concerning the difference between knowing the path and walking the path. He said, "Sooner or later you are going to realize, as I did, there's a difference between knowing the path and walking the path." For believers, this exhortation is only part of the puzzle. A more accurate exhortation might be: "Sooner or later you are going to realize as I did, there must be an integration of knowing the path and walking the path." The moment in time this occurs is the edge of incarnation. Whereas Morpheus' quote emphasizes the difference between the paths, Scripture emphasizes the integration of the paths (Matthew 7:15-23; James 1:22-25; Luke 6:46-49).
4. "The grace of God," used fifteen times in other NT passages—Romans. 5:15; 1 Corinthians 1:4; 3:10; 15:10; 2 Corinthians 1:12; 6:1; 8:1; 9:14; Galatians 2:21; Ephesians 3:2, 7: Colossians 1:6; 2 Thessalonians 1:12—gives strong evidence of reference to Christ's first coming, the incarnation. Later on, verse 13 complements this passage beautifully by describing the blessed hope found in the second Advent. "Paul says this grace 'has appeared,' ... by which he refers to its unique historical appearance in Christ, which is communicated in the Gospel, as it is implied in the words 'bringing salvation.' Synonyms for 'appear' in the passive tense are: 'to show oneself' or 'make an appearance.'" William Bauer, *A Greek-English Lexicon of the New Testament and Other Early Christian Literature* (Chicago: The University of Chicago Press, 1958).

"Forms of 'appeared' ... are used in Luke 1:78-79 and Acts 27:20 ('when for days on end neither sun nor stars appeared'). The Lord's face is referred to having appeared to His worshipers (Numbers 6:25; Psalms 30:7; 66:2; 79:4, 8). Because the phrase 'the grace of God' is non-Septuagintal, it is possible that the grace of God is meant to suggest His personal appearance." Jerome D. Quinn *Introduction to Titus, 1 and 2 Timothy the Pastoral Epistles* (The Anchor Bible Commentary, 1990).

The NIV and KJV differ from the NASB. {NIV—"For the grace of God that brings salvation has appeared to all men." KJV—"For the grace of God that bringeth salvation hath appeared to all men." NASB—"For the grace of God has appeared, bringing salvation to all men."} (BAGD 801) Verse 11 poses a problem, both theologically, grammatically, and lexically. Within this verse, a casual glance can build either doctrine of universal salvation or limited atonement.

In other passages in the NT, the word "saving" is defined as "salvation" (Luke 2:30, 3:6; Acts 28:28; Ephesians 6:17). Verse 11 is better translated: "God's grace made its appearance 'salvation-bringing.'" William Hendriksen, *New Testament Commentary: Titus* (Baker Book House: 2002).

In light of the different types or classes of people mentioned earlier (aged men, aged women, young men, younger men, even slaves {ver. 1-10}), God's saving power has been manifested to all alike. "All men" refers to "all classes of men, even slaves."

Some have built the doctrine of universal salvation from this passage and others. Should Romans 5:18 be interpreted that "every member of the human race is justified?" Should 1 Corinthians 15:22 be interpreted that "every member of the human race" is "made alive in Christ?"

Logically, if the nuance of universalistic is interpreted similarly in other passages, then:

(a) Every member of the human race regarded John the Baptist as a prophet (Mark 11:32).

(b) Every member of the human race wondered whether John was perhaps the Christ (Luke 3:15).

(c) Every member of the human race was searching for Jesus (Mark 1:37). Hendriksen, *Titus*.

Even in modern culture, within the English language, when referring to a collective group, one will use the term "everybody." It would be improper to assume universalistic nuances based on such a statement.

Therefore, it can be deduced from the following evidence that God's grace has made appearance with saving power to all classes of men. Wallace classifies the indirect object (all men) as a dative "after certain adjectives." Daniel B. Wallace, *Greek Grammar Beyond the Basics* (Grand Rapids: Zondervan Publishing House, 1996).

As a result, universal salvation is nowhere to be found in this passage. On the contrary, God's grace has been made available to all, but the appropriation of that grace is contingent upon the personal and individual faith placed upon that grace.

5. The present participle "instructing" ("giving guidance") in the NASB, "teaching" in the KJV and NIV, used in the original is from the same stem as is the noun pedagogue. Bauer, *Greek-English Lexicon*.

Here it is used in its Hellenistic sense, "the one who is educated." The noun speaks of a taskmaster, custodian, or slave whose job it was to conduct boys and youths to and from school and superintend their conduct generally. Martin Dibelius, *Pastoral Epistles* (Augsburg Fortress Publishers, 1972).

In classic literature, it was used in a sense to bring up, educate, instruct, teach, and accustom. "Derived from this noun paideia, which is found as early as the 6th century B.C. and which connotes the process of education, and development of culture." Colin Brown, *The New International Dictionary of New Testament Theology Vol. 1-4* (Grand Rapids: Zondervan Publishing House, 1975).

In the OT, *paideou* is used eighty-four times in the LXX, translated thirty-seven times for chastisement or discipline. God's education process for His children is not with an objective to pass a human test or remain intellectually sharpened. Rather, God's purpose in educating His people in the OT was that of faithfulness to the covenant relationship.

Originally God disciplined His people as a whole (Deuteronomy 4:36; 8:5; Hosea 7:12; 10:10). This discipline was later passed on to the individual (Proverbs 3:11). Finally, the education process was passed on to the father who acted as a family priest (Exodus 12:26; Deuteronomy 21:18; Proverbs 13:24).

In the NT, especially in Hebrews 12, discipline and chastisement is seen as a means of identification as a positional child of God. The author of Hebrews makes the logical connection that only fathers discipline their children. God, our Heavenly Father, disciplines with the purpose of establishing holiness in the lives of His children.

Specifically in Titus 2:11, the purpose (purpose participle) of God's grace teaches the believer how to live a sanctified life. The offer of justification is established and available in verse 11, and the outworking, purpose, and presence of that grace will teach, instruct, train, and guide the believer into specific aspect of holy living.

The concept of Christ, defined in Titus 2:11 as the grace of God, is applied in the congregational prayer of 1 Clem. 59:3: "through Jesus Christ through him you have taught us, made us holy, and brought us to honor." Dibelius, *The Pastoral Epistles*.

God's grace, that teaches and instructs, will result in believers "denying" ("disregard" BAGD 108)—aorist—result participle): (1) ungodliness and (2) worldly desires (NIV—"to say 'NO' to"; KJV—"denying"). The first things that will result from God's grace are negative in their action. The verb "deny" is translated "to say no to."

In classic literature, "arneomai" meant to reject, to refuse, or to decline. In the LXX and other Jewish literature, "arneomai" meant to despise, reject, renounce, or refuse (Wis. 12:27; 16:16; 17:10; 4 Mac. 8:7; 10:15). In the NT, "arneomai" (thirty-two times) {Acts, *Pastoral Epistles*, 1 and 2 Peter and Revelation}. Brown, *New International Dictionary*.

6. Therefore, the purpose of God's grace is to teach us, resulting in denying (renouncing, rejecting):

Ungodliness ("godlessness, impiety" BAGD 114) In classic literature it was translated as: outrage against someone, breaking laws, a misfit in behavior to the gods. In the OT, it was translated as: not fearing God, or His ordinances. In the NT, it was translated as: ungodliness, wickedness, sin, opposition to decency and orderliness.

Worldly desires (BAGD 293)—(NIV—"worldly passions"; KJV—"worldly lusts") In Classic Literature it was translated as: evils of this life, impulse, and desire. In the OT, occurring fifty times, it was translated as a morally indifferent desire (Deuteronomy 12:20), and an evil desire which is opposed to God's will (Numbers 11:4, 34; Deuteronomy 9:22). In the NT, desires can be found in every direction: sexual, material, and coveting another's possessions (Romans 1:24; 1 Timothy 6:9; Titus 3:3; Galatians 5:16-21). Verse 14 further defines worldly desires, "every lawless deed" (Brown Vol. 1 456-457). Brown, *New International Dictionary*.

7. Paul explains in the latter half of the verse three positive things regarding living that grace teaches. This positive living is stressing the beginning or entrance into the state of. {Aorist Ingressive} Wallace, *Greek Grammar*.

God's grace teaches us to live: sensibly. In classic literature it was translated figuratively and literally as: temperate minded, moderate, and self-controlled. In the OT, it was translated literally as: self-controlled, temperate, and moderation. Figuratively, it was translated as seize, restore, and master of emotions. In Koine Greek it was translated as: "to be sound minded" and "moderation." In the NT, it was translated literally as: sound judgment (Romans 12:3; 1 Peter 4:7; 2 Timothy 1:7), sound mind (2 Corinthians 5:13), encourage (Titus 2:4), temperate (1 Timothy 3:2), sensible (Titus 1:8, 2:2, 2:5, 2:6, 2:12), and self-restraint (1 Timothy 2:15). Figuratively, it is translated as discreetly (as in women's adorning) (1 Timothy 2:9), not out of mind (Acts 26:25).

Righteously ("uprightly"): In classic literature, it meant "one whose behavior fit into the framework of his society and who has fulfilled his rightful obligations towards the gods and his fellow man." Homer, *Odyssey*.

In the OT, righteousness is not conforming to legal standards, but conduct that is appropriate to the two way relationship between God and man. In the NT, specifically in the Pastoral Epistles, it is translated in its Hellenistic sense (1 Timothy 6:11; 2 Timothy 2:22; Titus 1:8). Paul translates it as "upright" in 1 Thessalonians 2:10. Brown, *New International Dictionary*.

Godly ("in a godly manner" BAGD 326): "In the 3rd and 4th century B.C. it denoted caution, circumspection, and discretion." Later on, it meant reverence (Liddel-Scott 720). In early Christian literature, it depicted discretion, fear, and reverence (Lampe 567). In the LXX, "eulabeomai" is translated as: "to take care of" (Brown Vol. 2 90). In the NT, it is translated as devout, God-fearing, and righteous. Brown, *New International Dictionary*.

In regards to the results ("denying"/"living") of what God's grace instructs the believer to do, Paul ends the verse by couching it in the context of this present world. This structuring of present tense sanctification complements the past reality of the incarnation in verse 11, and introduces the future reality of the second coming in verse 13.

8. Italics mine.

9. Galatians 5:1

10. John 5:19-27; Mark 6:33-44

11. John 12:1-2; Mark 11:27-33

12. John 11:43; Mark 6:31

13. It is interesting to notice that Peter warns his readers twice, with the end times in mind, to live balanced lives. Often, when thinking about end times, one can become completely unbalanced. It is easy then to be motivated by fear, instead of love. Therefore, gird your minds for action, keep sober *in spirit*, fix your hope completely on the grace to be brought to you at the revelation of Jesus Christ (1 Peter 1:13). The end of all things is at hand; therefore, be of sound judgment and sober* *spirit* for the purpose of prayer (1 Peter 4:7).

14. Lewis Carroll, *Alice in Wonderland* (Grosset & Dunlap, 1946).

15. Matthew 22:36-40

CHAPTER 4

1. Paul J. Achtemeier, *Harper Collins Bible Dictionary Revised Edition* (Society of Biblical Literature, 1996).

2. John 10:10

3. Obviously, this entire section is not referring to underage drinking. Associating oneself with illegal practices does not fall into the area of Christian liberty. We are told to obey governmental authorities (Romans 13:1). Alcoholic environments that perpetuate immorality or abuse should obviously be avoided as well. This section on alcohol is meant in reference to responsible and legal drinking.

4. 1 Timothy 3:3, 8; Titus 1:7

5. If we are honest, we all come to the Bible with preconceived notions. When we approach the Word, we need to ask the Holy Spirit to give us God's view on the issues at hand. Much evil has been justified through biblical passages taken out of context.

6. Dan Buck, "Getting out of the Faith Ghetto," RELEVANT magazine (March/April 2003).

7. 1 Timothy 4:8

8. 1 Corinthians 6:19-20

9. Matthew 28:19-20

10. God's first mission to Adam and Eve as a couple was to fill the earth (Genesis 1:28). God's first actual command to Adam (Eve was not yet created) is arguably the prohibition to eat the forbidden fruit (Genesis 2:16-17).

11. Matthew 28:19-20

12. *Discipleship Journal*, July/August 2003

13. Galatians 6:10

14. Matthew 5:13-16

15. Rocky Mountain Family Council, "Sacred vs. Secular" *http://www.rmfc.org/fs/fs0023.html*

16. Abraham Kuyper, "Abraham Kuyper" *http://www.redeemer.on.ca/academics/polisci/kuyper.html*

17. Jamie Bennett, "Relevant, but is it Ministry?" RELEVANT magazine *http://www.relevantmagazine.com*

18. Michael S. Horton, *Where in the World is the Church?* (Phillipsburg, New Jersey: R&R Publishing, 1995 & 2002).

19. 1 Corinthians 6:12; Philippians 4:8-9

20. Acts 17:11

21. Galatians 3:21-24

22. Emphasis mine

23. Isaiah 1:11

24. Deuteronomy 6:4

25. Matthew 9:13

26. Please realize that the following section is in regard to issues of "Christian liberty." By that phrase I am referring to those issues that are not strictly forbidden in Scripture. In reality, a considerable amount of issues fall under this category. In Paul's day, some of these pressing issues were: food sacrificed to idols, eating and drinking, taking a wife, refraining from working, eating only vegetables, and regarding one day above another. That which counters the Bible is out of the question.

CHAPTER 5

1. If we are honest, we all come to the Bible with preconceived notions. When we approach the Word, we need to ask the Holy Spirit to give us God's view on the issues at hand. Much evil has been justified through biblical passages taken out of context.

2. We will look at exactly how to do this in Chapter 10, "A Global Movement."

3. This paragraph is loosely inspired by a talk given by Joshua Harris.

4. *http://www.geocites.com/bruneydgirl16/QuotesCourage.html*

CHAPTER 6

1. Carroll, *Alice*.

2. Hebrews 11:4; 1 John 3:11-12

3. Acts 9:3-4

4. 1 Corinthians 9:22

5. 1 Corinthians 9:26-27

6. Galatians 1:17. John MacArthur, *The MacArthur New Testament Commentary: Galatians* (Moody Publishers, 1987).

7. Strabo (xiv.6,73)

8. Sir William M. Ramsay, *The Cities of St. Paul: Their Influence on His Life and Thought* (London: Hodder & Stoughton, 1907).

9. James 1:21

10. Acts 17:14-34

11. Acts 17:17

12. Acts 17:22

13. Acts 17:23

CHAPTER 7

1. Taken from *Essay On Love*.

2. *http://www.howe.k12.ok.us/~jimaskew/bbones.htm*

3. Millard J. Erickson, *Christian Theology* (Grand Rapids: Baker Book House, 1983).

4. Dichotomy is derived from two Greek roots: *diche*, meaning "twofold" or "into two," and *temnein*, meaning "to cut." John B. Woodward, *Man as Spirit, Soul, and Body* (Chapter 3 "Theological Models of Man's Makeup") *http://www.gracenotebook.com/trichotomy_ch_3.htm*

5. Trichotomy is derived from two Greek roots: *tricha*, meaning "three," and *temno*, meaning "to cut." Paul Enns, *The Moody Handbook of Theology* (Chicago: Moody Press, 1989).

6. The supporting verses for each of the models (monism, dichotomy, trichotomy) are numerous. Although, Paul only mentions three parts (body, soul, and spirit) in 1 Thessalonians 5:23, several more parts are mentioned in other passages. In Deuteronomy 6:5, Moses seems to be referring to a trichotomy of sorts. However, he mentions two terms (heart and might) that Paul failed to mention. Perhaps, by combining Moses' list with Paul's list, maybe man is really made up of five parts. This supports the model called pentachotomy (Gary F. Zeolla, "Soul, Spirit, and Knowing God" Part Two *http://www.dtl.org/dtl/treatise/soul-spirit-2.htm*).

7. The conversation of how many parts make up a person is significant and relevant in many aspects of theological study. It is both interesting and informative. I believe that in our journey towards a transformed mind, the sticking point is not whether or not a person believes in dichotomy or septachotomy. The significant point is how the many parts of a person connect and relate in one's holistic love for God.

In other words, a partial and segmented love for God will prove to be theologically incorrect and detrimental towards maintaining the life of a transformist. It is impossible to be relevant when one only loves God with an aspect of himself or herself.

Additional sources listed below are for the reader who desires to study more about the specific parts that make up an individual.

Gordon H. Clark, *The Biblical Doctrine of Man* (Jefferson, MD: The Trinity Foundation, 1984).

Lewis S. Chafer, *Systematic Theology* (Dallas: Dallas Seminary Press, 1947).

William H. Baker, *Survey of Theology II*, Lesson 5 (Moody Bible Institute, 1990).

http://www.gracenotebook.com/trichotomy_ch_3.htm

http://www.gracenotebook.com/trichotomy_ch_6.htm

http://www.gracenotebook.com/trichotomy_ch_7.htm

8. Mark 12:30; Luke 10:27

9. Woodward, *Man*.

10. "Your Mind Your Body," Michael D. Lemonick, *Time* (January, 20 2003).

11. Ibid.

12. Luke 7:44-50

13. For further study, please read anything by John Eldredge. God has allowed his writings to expose and heal my heart. I especially recommend: Brent Curtis and John Eldredge's *The Sacred Romance* (Thomas Nelson Publishers: 1997).

14. Read John 13:1-8. Peter seemed to be presenting himself in a manner of humility. Jesus exposed His heart and the pride that temporarily characterized it.

15. Proverbs 14:12; 16:26

16. Genesis 4:6; Jonah 4:3

17. LDS Apostle James E. Talmage, *Articles of Faith*, LDS Collectors Library '97 CD-ROM Ch.24, p.430 - p.431.

18. Genesis 4:5; Leviticus 10:1-2; 1 Samuel 15:22-23

19. Exodus 20:3

20. Matthew 16:22; John 13:6-10; Acts 10:14

21. Matthew 4:19, 8:22, 9:9, 10:38, 16:24, 19:21; Mark 1:17, 2:14, 8:34, 10:21; Luke 5:27, 9:23, 9:59, 18:22; John 1:43, 10:27, 12:26, 13:36, 21:19, 21:22.

22. Fisherman owned their own ships, took hirelings into their service, and sometimes joined together to form companies. Bromiley, ISBE.

23. Luke 9:49, 54; John 18:10

24. The Sea of Galilee (named from the district), otherwise known as the "Lake of Gennesaret," comes from a plain on its northwest shore (cf. Matt 14:34), or the "Sea of Tiberias." It was subject to violent squalls and supported flourishing fisheries. Frank E. Gaebelin, *The Expositor's Bible Commentary*, (Grand Rapids: Zondervan Publishing House, CD-ROM).

25. There were several important centers of fishing and fish industry along the shore of Lake Tiberias, as attested by the names Bethsaida ("house of fishing"), Magdala ("bulwark of the fishes"), and Tarichaea ("salting installation for fish"). Bromiley, ISBE.

26. Greek has several expressions for "follow me" (v. 19; cf. at 10:38; Luke 9:23, 14:27), but they all presuppose a physical "following" during Jesus' ministry. His "followers" were not just "hearers"; they actually followed their Master around (as students then did) and became, as it were, trainees. The Greek word for "follow me" is used by Matthew several times in reference to discipleship (8:22, 10:38, 16:24, 19:21, 19:28). Gaebelin, *The Expositor's Bible Commentary*.

27. Jesus' phrase "fishers of men" is probably referring to the passage in Jeremiah 16:16. W. F. Albright and C.C. Mann, *The Anchor Bible—Matthew* (New York: Doubleday & Company Inc., 1971).

28. There is a straight line from this commission to the Great Commission (28:18-20). Jesus' followers are indeed to catch men. Gaebelin, *The Expositor's Bible Commentary*.

29. Most likely Zebedee, the father of James and John, had desires to pass on the business to his two aggressive sons who were very capable. It could easily be reckoned that James and John, ever since growing up as children, were told that they would be fishermen. In that age of apprentices and disciples, boys would often focus on a trade or business and study under a father or mentor in aims of one day taking over it.

30. Luke adds more detail compared to Matthew. In the Luke 5:1-11 account, Jesus performs a miracle with fish that authenticates the authority of His call in the preceding verses. As the result of this miracle catch, Peter, James, and John (Andrew not mentioned) leave all they know to follow the One who knows them. Douglass R. Hare, *Interpretation—Matthew* (Louisville: John Knox Press, 1993).

31. Simon and Andrew were casting a "net" (*amphiblestron*, a NT hapax legomenon [found only once], with a cognate at Mark 1:16). It refers to a circular "casting-net" and is not to be confused with the more generic term *diktua* in 4:20. Gaebelin, *The Expositor's Bible Commentary*.

32. Mark 1:29-31 Mark's account of healing Peter's mother-in-law is placed before the call to discipleship in Luke (4:38-39). Jesus was already famous for his miracles (Luke 4:37), and thus Matthew's account can seem misleading, with the disciples leaving everything before they ever knew anything of Jesus. Hare, *Interpretation—Matthew*.

33. Matthew 19:27

34. If the miracle of Luke 5:1-11 occurred the night before Matthew 4:18-22 (Mark 1:16-20), that would be another reason for their immediate response to Jesus. Gaebelin, *The Expositor's Bible Commentary*.

35. About February of the year A.D. 27, the first call of discipleship was given to Andrew. He brought his brother Simon (Peter) to Jesus. Although occasionally accompanying Christ on His trips, the disciples are thought to have continued with their secular occupations. The call listed in Matthew 4:18-22 is about a year later, February A.D. 28. At this point they appear to be consistent companions of Christ. By this time, although details are very limited in Matthew, it has been a full year since Jesus renamed Peter in John 1:35-42. The disciples, who initially made a huge decision to follow Jesus, had much training to undergo. They initially lacked spiritual sensitivity (Matthew 13:6, 15:33, 16:7-12, 16:22-23, 17:10-13, 19:10-12, 19:23-30, 24:3), sympathy (14:15-16, 23; 19:13-15), humility (18:1-4), forgiveness (18:21, 22), perseverance in prayer (17:16-21), and courage (26:56, 69-75). William Hendriksen, *New Testament Commentary—Matthew*, (Grand Rapids: Baker Book House, 1973).

36. Matthew 9:9

37. "Immediately" conveys an action not contingent upon convenience. It is used eleven times in Matthew. Brown, *The New International Dictionary*.

38. "Weight" refers to a burden or impediment. It doesn't refer to sin or evil necessarily. Rather, it conveys something that will inhibit an athlete in competition. "Everything that hinders" translates *onkos* (only here in the NT), a word that may mean any kind of weight. Bauer, *A Greek-English Lexicon*.

39. Paul considered all things to be a loss, damage, or forfeit compared to knowing Christ. By using "all things" rather than "these things," (v. 7), Paul's thought broadens from his Jewish advantages just mentioned to include everything that might conceivably be a rival to his total trust in Christ.

40. Genesis 22

41. Matthew 19:27-30

CHAPTER 8

1. John 4:1-43
2. Ralph Turnball, *The Minister's Obstacles.*
3. Isaiah 64:6
4. Romans 7:18
5. Isaiah 53:6
6 Proverbs 14:12, 16:25
7. 1 Peter 1:14-16
8. Romans 8:32; 2 Timothy 3:16-17
9. Titus 1:2
10. Romans 8:38-39
11. 2 Corinthians 5:17
12. John 13:14-15; Hebrews 6:20
13. Mark 9:34; Luke 9:46; and Luke 22:24
14. John Eldredge, *Wild at Heart* (Nashville: Thomas Nelson, 2001).
15. Jeremiah 17:9
16. Ezekiel 36:26

CHAPTER 9

1. Carl F. H. Henry, *Toward a Recovery of Christian Belief* (Westchester: Crossway Books, 1990).
2. Clark Pinnock, *Destruction of the Finally Impenitent* (1990).
3. Job 1:20-21, 2:3,10
4. Job 38-41
5. Isaiah 53:6, Romans 3:10, 23
6. Colossians 2:6-10
7. Romans 10:17
8. Philippians 3:17, 4:9; 1 Corinthians 4:16; 1 Thessalonians 1:6; 2 Thessalonians 3:9
9. Acts 17:16
10. Acts 17:17
11. Hebrew 6:1-2
12. Galatians 1:6-9
13. Luke 24:27; Acts 8:35; Acts 26:22; 28:23
14. Thanks Mike Jentes.
15. John 4:29
16. 1 Peter 2:2; John 4:29
17. Even Paul, the seasoned saint, learned a vital lesson. He was so against John Mark joining the missionary efforts that he forbid him to come. John Mark deserted him once before and he was not going to take any chances again (Acts 15:37-40). Later in his ministry though, Paul recognized that John Mark was useful (2 Timothy 4:11). I guess we all make mistakes.

CHAPTER 10

1. *http://www.landingplace.org*
2. *http://www.columbusunderground.com/reviews/shortnorth.shtml*
3. *http://www.tripadvisor.com/Attraction_Review-g50226-d183839-Reviews-Short_North-Columbus_Ohio.html*
4. *http://www.woodcompanies.com/History.htm*

CHAPTER 11

1. 1 Kings 3:9
2. 1 Kings 2:4
3 I Kings 11:11
4. *Merriam-Webster, Merriam-Webster's Collegiate Dictionary, 11th Edition* (Merriam-Webster, Inc: July 2003).
5. Ibid.

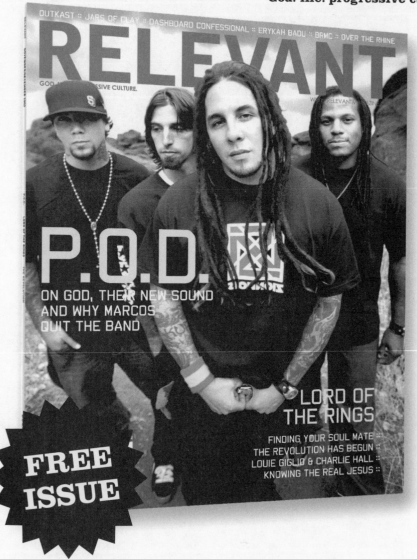